Limerick County Library

30012 00667399

WITHDRAWN FROM STOCK

D0190832

Neven's Real Food

for families

WITHDRAWN FROM STOCK

WITHDRAWN FROM STOCK

Neven's
Real Food

for families

LIMERICK
COUNTY LIBRARY
00667299
WITHDRAWN
FROM STOCK

641.5

Neven Maguire

GILL & MACMILLAN

Gill & Macmillan Ltd
Hume Avenue
Park West
Dublin 12
with associated companies throughout the world
www.gillmacmillan.ie

© Neven Maguire 2007

978 07171 4261 3

Compiled by Orla Broderick

Photographs by Hugh McElveen

Food styled by Sharon Hearne-Smith

Props supplied by Avoca, Dunnes Stores,
Habitat, House of Fraser, Arnotts and Murphy Sheehy

Index compiled by Cover to Cover

Book design and typesetting by Anú Design

Printed by GraphyCems Ltd, Spain

The paper used in this book is made from the wood pulp of managed forests. For every
tree felled, at least one tree is planted, thereby renewing natural resources.

All rights reserved. No part of this publication may be copied, reproduced or transmitted
in any form or by any means without permission of the publishers.

A CIP catalogue record is available for this book from the British Library.

To my Auntie Maureen for all her support,
both loving and inspiring. But most of all for being there
as a friend and teaching me the art of good food.

Contents

Everyday Suppers

Baking in the Afternoon

SPECIAL OCCASION MENUS

St Patrick's Day Lunch

Easter Lunch

Christmas Dinner

Al Fresco Lunch

AFTER EIGHT OCCASIONS

St Valentine's Dinner

Acknowledgments

It's always difficult to know where to start when it comes to acknowledgments. There are those who are directly involved in the book, but I certainly can't forget the producers and suppliers who make my job so much easier. So thanks again to my local butcher Kevin McGovern; Ken Moffitt who supplies my free-range poultry; Peter Curry for spanking fresh seafood; McDaids for excellent Irish fruit and vegetables; to Mark, Samantha and Hugh at B.D. Foods, Monaghan; Rod at Eden Plants, Co. Leitrim; Ernst at Barbizon Herbs and Eoin O'Flynn and John Martin from Flogas.

It was once again a pleasure to work with Orla Broderick, who helped me compile this book. Thanks to Sharon Hearne-Smith for her energy, enthusiasm and attention to detail in doing the food styling. To Hugh McElveen for creating the fabulous photographs that accompany the recipes in my book. To Sarah Liddy, my commissioning editor, who kept me focused even during the run up to my marriage and opening of the refurbished restaurant. Thanks also to Emma Farrell, Nicki Howard, Kristin Jensen and the rest of the team at Gill & Macmillan, who really know how to produce books that people genuinely use.

To my agent John Masterson for keeping me straight and for being endlessly supportive and to his colleagues at Purcell Masterson, Mary Tallent, Naoimh Murphy and Aoife Keane.

To Amelda, my wonderful new wife, without whose constant backup in the business and feedback on recipes I would never have been able to achieve so much. And to my wonderful chefs in the kitchen, Glen Wheeler, Declan Greene and Laura Mullen, without whom this book would never have happened.

Thanks also to Michael and Margaret Heffernan of Dunnes Stores and their team, especially Roisin Devlin, Lynda O'Keeffe and John Hickey. I have enjoyed working with them immensely this year and appreciate all the help they have given me on this particular project.

Last but by no means least I'd like to thank Vera my mother and all the family for always being there for me.

Introduction

It's great to know how many of you have enjoyed my previous books. I love to get your feedback and it seems that everyone wants the same things when it comes to recipes: good, delicious, nutritious meals that are easy and straightforward to prepare and guaranteed to have everyone coming back for seconds.

Meal times in our home have never followed a pattern and I hope that this book reflects this. Sometimes we find ourselves with a bowl of pasta, relaxing in front of the TV after a long night's service in the restaurant, while other times the house is packed with our extended family all expecting to be fed. From one day to the next, family meals vary, not just in the time of day, but who's eating and how long you've got to prepare the meal. Weekends are everyone's favourite time of the week (unless, of course, you happen to be working). For most people, it's a time to relax, a time to enjoy the family, a time for fun and a time to enjoy good food without the mid-week rush.

After breakfast on a Saturday, I love to take a stroll around a farmers' market to see what's on offer, to look at great local produce and to remind myself of the huge benefits of eating in season. As far as I'm concerned, it's time to get back to seasonal eating – for me personally it makes sense to eat light summery salads and vegetables in the summer and earthy root vegetables during the winter.

I've tried to structure this book so that you can find a feel-good fix for every occasion. This could be a much-needed brunch when you wake up with a house full of guests after a big night out, or a simple supper when you're tired and hungry with only an hour to spare. I have divided the book into sections that reflect the range of occasions that you might want to cater for: 'Breakfasts', with lots of yummy dishes to kick off the day; 'Soups and Lunches', full of new and exciting ways to get through the day; 'Everyday Suppers', for that effortless tasty meal mid-week; and 'Baking in the Afternoon', to get us back into the kitchen with or without the children.

The section with Special Occasion menus are for all the important times in our lives: 'St Patrick's Day Lunch', 'Easter Lunch', 'Christmas Dinner', 'Al Fresco Lunch', 'St Valentine's Dinner', 'Anniversary Dinner', '*Late Late Toy Show*' and 'Movie Night'. All of these times have great significance and importance for us and our families. They are the times we look forward to and often plan in great detail. Of course, you can mix and match the dishes, but I hope whatever the occasion, you'll be able to pick up this book and find recipes that fit the bill.

There are healthy, balanced meals in the 'Breakfast', 'Soups and Lunches' and 'Everyday Suppers' chapters, but of course, there are also chapters for that something special, be it preparing an extravagant menu for an important family celebration or treating yourself to the time to make one of the recipes from the 'Baking in the Afternoon' chapter on a rainy day.

Everyday
eating

Things to Note

- I always use Irish meat so that I know it is quality assured and regulated by Bord Bia.

- Where possible, use organic eggs, though free-range are another good alternative.

- Wipe off any excess dirt from mushrooms – never wash them, as they can become waterlogged.

- I always pay that little extra for free-range Irish chicken so that I'm confident about what I'm eating.

- I prefer to use the Thai Gold brand of coconut milk and curry paste.

- A selection of recipes were exclusively published in the *RTÉ Guide* and have been tried and tested by *RTÉ Guide* readers.

Where you see

RTÉ GUIDE

READER TESTED these recipes have received a stamp of approval.

Breakfast

Breakfast bar

This is a winning breakfast for children and adults alike. As dried fruit and nuts are an excellent source of energy, they should keep everyone happy until lunchtime. Eat in the car if you are planning an early start or use for lunchboxes or picnics as an excellent healthy option. Experiment by replacing the sultanas with dried cranberries, cherries or banana chips. Leave out the peanut butter and almonds if you have any doubt about a nut allergy.

Makes 16 bars

150 g (5 oz) porridge oats
50 g (2 oz) sultanas
75 g (3 oz) ready-to-eat apricots, chopped
50 g (2 oz) dried papaya, finely chopped
50 g (2 oz) dates, pitted
25 g (1 oz) flaked almonds
25 g (1 oz) sesame seeds
2 tablespoons clear honey
3 tablespoons smooth peanut butter
1 egg white

Preheat the oven to 190°C/350°F/gas 5 and line a 27 ½ cm x 18 cm (11 inch x 7 inch) baking tin with non-stick parchment paper. Place the porridge oats in a bowl and stir in the sultanas, apricots, papaya, dates, flaked almonds and sesame seeds.

Place the honey and peanut butter in a small pan and heat gently, stirring occasionally until smooth. Drizzle into the oat mixture and mix well to combine.

Put the egg white in a bowl and beat with a balloon whisk until light and frothy. Fold into the oat and honey mixture until everything is sticking together. Transfer to the prepared baking tin and spread out evenly, pressing down the mixture with the back of a spoon to make the surface as even as possible.

Bake for 15–20 minutes, until the top is golden brown and feels firm to the touch. Remove from the oven and cool slightly in the tin, then cut into 16 bars. Leave to cool completely before removing them from the tin. Store the bars in an airtight container for up to 5 days.

Apple muffins

These are not muffins in the strictest sense of the word, as they don't rise as much. However, they are wonderfully dense and moist, perfect for a nutritious breakfast. Serve them on the day that they are made or wrap in cling film and freeze for up to 1 month.

Makes 12

75 g (3 oz) self-raising flour
2 teaspoons baking powder
1 teaspoon mixed spice
50 g (2 oz) wheat bran (such as Odlums)
50 g (2 oz) light muscovado sugar
50 g (2 oz) sultanas
2 eating apples, peeled, cored and finely chopped
25 g (1 oz) pecan nuts, chopped
50 g (2 oz) dates, pitted and chopped
100 ml (3 ½ fl oz) sunflower oil
2 eggs
2 tablespoons natural yoghurt
1 teaspoon sesame seeds

RTÉ **GUIDE**

READER TESTED

Preheat the oven to 200°C/400°F/gas 6. Line a muffin tin with 12 deep paper cases. Sift the flour, baking powder and mixed spice into a bowl. Tip in the bran left in the sieve and stir in with the wheat bran.

Add the sugar to the flour mixture with the sultanas, apples, pecans and dates and mix lightly with a wooden spoon. Measure the oil out in a jug, break in the eggs and add the yoghurt, then lightly beat to combine. Make a well in the centre of the dry ingredients and pour in the oil mixture. Stir lightly until just mixed (don't over-mix).

Spoon the mixture equally into paper cases until two-thirds full. Sprinkle sesame seeds over the top. Bake for 16–18 minutes, until golden brown and firm to the touch. Leave to cool for 5 minutes, then serve warm.

Variations

Banana and date muffins

Replace the apples with two ripe mashed bananas and use extra chopped pitted dates instead of sultanas. Sprinkle the tops with a little Demerara sugar.

Blueberry, coconut and lemon

Use 175 g (6 oz) blueberries instead of the apples, sultanas and dates.
Replace the pecan nuts with 40 g (1 ½ oz) desiccated coconut and add in the finely grated rind of 1 lemon.

Muesli

This is a great recipe to get the children involved, and the best part is that they will be much more likely to eat it for their breakfast! Get them to roll up their sleeves and use a teacup to measure the different ingredients. To make this into a fruit granola, drizzle the porridge oats with 2 tablespoons each of sunflower oil and brown sugar or maple syrup before baking.

Serves 10–12

450 g (1 lb) porridge oats
50 g (2 oz) flaked almonds
50 g (2 oz) sunflower seeds
50 g (2 oz) pumpkin seeds
50 g (2 oz) whole skinned hazelnuts, chopped
50 g (2 oz) wheat germ
100 g (4 oz) ready-to-eat dried apricots, chopped
50 g (2 oz) dried banana chips
50 g (2 oz) golden sultanas
50 g (2 oz) dried cranberries
25 g (1 oz) linseed (optional)
sliced banana, halved strawberries and/or seedless grapes, to garnish
cold milk or natural yoghurt, to serve

Preheat the oven to 200°C/400°F/gas 6. Spread the porridge oats out on a baking sheet. On a separate baking sheet, sprinkle over the flaked almonds, sunflower seeds, pumpkin seeds and hazelnuts and place on the top shelf of the oven with the porridge oats underneath. Bake for 5 minutes, until lightly toasted, tossing occasionally so that they cook evenly. Remove from the oven and leave to cool.

Once cool, place the toasted porridge oats, nuts and seeds in a large bowl. Stir in the wheat germ with the apricots, banana chips, sultanas, cranberries and linseed, if using. Transfer to a large Kilner jar or rigid plastic container and seal tightly with a lid.

To serve, spoon some muesli into a cereal bowl and scatter the sliced banana, strawberries and/or grapes on top to garnish. Pour over milk or add a good dollop of yoghurt.

Brown wheaten bread

This is the first thing we make every morning at the restaurant so that the guests who have stayed overnight wake up to the smell wafting around the house. It is delicious sprinkled with a couple of tablespoons of sesame seeds or sunflower seeds before baking. If you don't have any buttermilk in the house, sour ordinary milk with the juice of a lemon.

Makes 3 loaves

rapeseed or sunflower oil, for greasing
450 g (1 lb) plain flour, plus extra for dusting
450 g (1 lb) coarse wholemeal flour
1 teaspoon baking soda
1 teaspoon salt
100 g (4 oz) wheat bran (such as Odlums)
50 g (2 oz) butter
1 tablespoon golden syrup
1 tablespoon light muscovado sugar
600 ml (1 pint) buttermilk, plus a little extra if necessary
butter for spreading, to serve

Preheat the oven to 180°C/350°F/gas 5 and lightly oil 3 x 900 ml (1 ½ pint) loaf tins. Sift the flours, baking soda and salt into a bowl. Tip in the bran left in the sieve and stir in with the wheat bran. Rub in the butter with your fingertips until evenly dispersed.

Make a well in the centre of the dry ingredients and add the golden syrup, sugar and buttermilk. Using a large spoon, mix gently and quickly until you have achieved a nice dropping consistency. Add a little bit more buttermilk if necessary until the dough binds together without being sloppy.

Divide the dough into three equal pieces and place in the prepared loaf tins. Bake for 25 minutes, then check that the loaves are not browning too much. If they are, reduce the temperature or move the loaves down in the oven, then bake for a further 20 minutes until cooked through and each one has a slightly cracked top.

To check the loaves are properly cooked, tip each one out of the tin and tap the base. It should sound hollow. If it doesn't, return it to the oven for another 5 minutes. Tip out onto a wire rack and leave to cool completely. To serve, place the brown wheaten bread on a bread board and cut into slices at the table. Hand around with a separate pot of butter for spreading.

Variations

Scones

On a lightly floured surface, lightly roll out the dough to a 2 cm (¾ inch) thickness and cut into rounds with a 6 cm (2 ½ inch) plain cutter. Bake at 220°C/425°F/gas 7 for 10–15 minutes, until golden brown and well risen.

White soda bread

Replace the wholemeal flour and wheat bran and use all plain flour.

Light brown soda bread

Use about three-quarters plain flour to one-quarter coarse wholemeal flour and add 25 g (1 oz) of pinhead oatmeal before adding the buttermilk.

Poached eggs with buttered muffins, ham and sautéed spinach

This is a variation on classic eggs Benedict, a perfect breakfast dish. If you are going to be short of time in the morning, prepare the poached eggs the day before, as they sit perfectly happily in the fridge. Omit the ham for a great vegetarian option and serve with some roasted cherry tomatoes that have been cooked on the vine.

Serves 4

1 tablespoon white wine vinegar
4 eggs
40 g (1 ½ oz) unsalted butter
350 g (12 oz) baby spinach leaves
2 white muffins, split in half
225 g (8 oz) hand-carved cooked ham, trimmed

For the butter sauce
50 ml (2 fl oz) cream
1 teaspoon Dijon mustard
1 teaspoon softened butter
1 teaspoon snipped fresh chives, plus extra to garnish
salt and freshly ground black pepper

Heat a large pan with 2 ¼ litres (4 pints) water. Add the white wine vinegar and bring to the boil. Break each egg into the water where it is bubbling, then move the pan to the edge of the heat and simmer gently for 3 minutes. Remove the eggs with a slotted spoon and plunge into a bowl of iced water. When cold, trim down any ragged ends from the cooked egg white. These will keep happily in the fridge for up to 24 hours.

When ready to serve, preheat the grill. Add half of the butter to a large pan and once it starts to foam, tip in the spinach. Sauté over a fairly high heat until just wilted. Season to taste and drain off any excess liquid on kitchen paper. Keep warm. Arrange the muffin halves on a grill pan, cut side up, and cook for 2–3 minutes, until lightly toasted. Spread with the remaining butter.

Meanwhile, bring a large pan of salted water to the boil. Add the poached eggs and cook for 1–2 minutes to warm through. To make the butter sauce, place the cream and mustard in a small pan and simmer for 1 minute. Whisk in the butter and stir in the chives. Season to taste and keep warm.

To serve, place the muffins on warmed plates and spoon on small mounds of the spinach, then arrange the ham on top. Using a slotted spoon, remove the poached eggs from the pan and drain briefly on kitchen paper. Place on top of the ham and spoon over the butter sauce. Sprinkle over the chives to garnish.

Scrambled eggs with hot smoked salmon

If you prefer your scrambled eggs more chunky, do not whisk the egg and cream mixture – pour or break the eggs straight into the pan and then add the cream, stirring continuously. I much prefer to fold in the hot smoked salmon at the very end of cooking to keep its texture.

Serves 4

6 eggs
3 tablespoons milk
1 tablespoon snipped fresh chives
40 g (1 ½ oz) butter
175 g (6 oz) hot smoked salmon, skinned and flaked
4 slices multi-grain bread
salt and freshly ground black pepper
fresh long chives, to garnish (optional)

Preheat the grill. Whisk together the eggs, milk, chives and plenty of freshly ground black pepper. Heat a knob of the butter in a non-stick frying pan until foaming. Add the egg mixture and whisk continuously for 2–3 minutes, until just set but still soft. Remove from the heat, as they will continue to cook, and gently fold in the hot smoked salmon. Check the seasoning and add a pinch of salt if you think it needs it.

Meanwhile, toast the bread on a grill rack, then spread each piece of toast with the remaining butter and cut into triangles. Arrange two of the toasted bread triangles on each warmed plate and top each one with the scrambled eggs and hot smoked salmon. Garnish with the chives to serve.

French omelette with smoked bacon

Omelettes are so quick that it's not worth cooking a large one for two. Don't over-beat the eggs, as it will spoil the texture. A combination of wild mushrooms, which most supermarkets are now stocking, would make this into a very special breakfast.

Serves 1

RTÉ **GUIDE**

READER TESTED

2 teaspoons sunflower oil
1 large flat mushroom, sliced into small pieces
1 smoked streaky bacon rasher, rind removed and chopped
2 eggs
1 tablespoon chopped fresh flat-leaf parsley
knob unsalted butter
50 g (2 oz) Gruyère or Cheddar cheese, thinly sliced (optional)
salt and freshly ground black pepper
crusty French bread, to serve

Preheat the grill and heat a non-stick frying pan with a base about 20 cm (8 inches) in diameter. Add half of the oil and tip in the mushroom and bacon. Season to taste, then sauté for 2–3 minutes, until tender. Tip into a bowl and set aside.

Wipe out the frying pan and return to the hob. Break the eggs into a bowl and add the parsley, then season and lightly beat. When the pan is hot, add the remaining oil and then the butter, swirling it around so that the base and sides get coated.

While the butter is still foaming, pour in the egg mixture, tilting the pan from side to side. Stir gently with a fork or wooden spatula, drawing the mixture from the sides to the centre as it sets. When the eggs have almost set, scatter over the cheese, if using, and place under the grill for 1–2 minutes, until the omelette has set and the cheese has melted.

Scatter the reserved mushroom and bacon mixture over the grilled omelette and tilt the pan away from you slightly. Use a palette knife to fold over a third of the omelette to the centre, then fold over the opposite third. Slide onto a warmed plate, allowing it to flip over so that the folded sides are underneath. Serve at once with some crusty bread.

Chorizo and
new potato tortilla

Perfect for brunch, this recipe is a variation on the original Spanish tortilla. Once it has cooked, it should be golden brown on the outside but still succulent and moist in the middle. Tortilla makes a great breakfast centrepiece, or, because it is also excellent served cold, it makes fantastic picnic food cut into wedges and wrapped in cling film.

Serves 4

3 tablespoons olive oil
1 large onion, thinly sliced
225 g (8 oz) small new potatoes, scrubbed
175 g (6 oz) raw chorizo, peeled and thinly sliced
6 eggs
1 tablespoon chopped fresh flat-leaf parsley
salt and freshly ground black pepper
lightly dressed green salad, to serve (optional)

Heat 2 tablespoons of the oil in a non-stick frying pan with a base that is 17 cm (6 ½ inches) in diameter. Add the onion and sauté for about 5 minutes, until softened but not coloured.

Thinly slice the potatoes into ½ cm (¼ inch) slices. Dry in a clean tea towel and add to the pan, tossing to combine. Season generously, reduce the heat and cover with a lid or flat plate, then cook gently for 10–15 minutes, until almost tender. Turn them over once or twice and shake the pan occasionally to ensure they cook evenly.

Add the chorizo to the pan and cook for another 3 minutes or so, until the potatoes are tender and the chorizo is sizzling and its colour has begun to bleed into the potatoes.

Break the eggs into a large bowl and add the parsley and a good pinch of seasoning, then whisk lightly with a fork. When the potato and chorizo mixture is cooked, drain off any excess oil and then quickly stir into the beaten eggs.

Wipe out the pan and use to heat the remaining tablespoon of oil. Tip in the potato and egg mixture, pressing it down gently, and reduce the heat to the lowest setting. Cook for 15–20 minutes. When there is virtually no raw egg mixture left on top of the omelette, invert onto a flat plate.

Slide the omelette back into the pan and cook for another 5 minutes. Turn off the heat and set aside for 5 minutes to finish cooking. It should be cooked through but still moist in the centre.

To serve warm or cold, turn the tortilla onto a chopping board and cut into four wedges. Place a wedge on each plate with a small mound of salad if liked and serve at once.

The MacNean special breakfast

This is a simplified version of the full Irish that we serve to guests. Normally there's some boiled boxty with it and a slice of pan-fried pork liver. It's important to me that it leaves a marked impression, as it's the last thing customers have to eat before they leave. It is not as easy as it looks, so it needs a bit of clever timing if the results are going to be perfect. Obviously, you could grill everything for a healthier option.

Serves 4

4–8 pork and leek sausages (preferably made by a craft butcher)
sunflower oil, for frying
2 ripe vine tomatoes, halved
butter, for grilling and frying
4 slices each black and white pudding (preferably Clonakilty)
4 rindless back bacon rashers (preferably dry cured)
4 potato bread farls
225 g (8 oz) flat or field mushrooms, chopped
4 eggs
salt and freshly ground black pepper

Preheat the oven to 150°C/300°F/gas 2 and preheat the grill. Heat a large heavy-based frying pan. Fry the sausages in a little sunflower oil over a medium heat, turning every now and then, for 8–10 minutes, until cooked through. Put onto a baking sheet and slide into the oven to keep hot.

Arrange the tomatoes cut side up on a grill rack, dot each one with a little butter and season to taste. Place the black and white puddings alongside and grill for 4–5 minutes, turning the puddings once, then keep warm with the sausages.

Meanwhile, wipe out the frying pan, add a teaspoon or two of oil and fry the bacon for 1–2 minutes on each side, until crisp and golden brown. Keep warm with the sausages, black and white puddings and tomatoes.

Heat another tablespoon of oil with the bacon fat left in the frying pan, add the potato bread farls and fry for 1–2 minutes on each side, until crisp and golden. Put onto a second baking tray and slide into the oven.

Meanwhile, melt a small knob of butter in a separate medium frying pan, add the mushrooms and season to taste, then cook over a high heat for 2–3 minutes. Set to one side.

Wipe the frying pan clean again, heat a thin layer of oil in it over a medium-high heat and break in the eggs. Season to taste and fry for a couple of minutes, spooning a little of the hot fat over the yolks, until they are just set.

To serve, arrange the sausages on warmed plates with the tomatoes, black and white puddings, bacon and mushrooms. Arrange the fried potato bread farls to one side and place a fried egg on top of each one to serve.

Fried eggs on ciabatta with crispy pancetta

Ciabatta is an Italian loaf – its shape is supposed to resemble a slipper. It should have large holes and a soft but chewy, floury crust. Pancetta is the Italian version of smoked streaky bacon but tends to be a little thinner and always goes wonderfully crisp. However, if you have any difficulty getting hold of it, simply use rindless smoked streaky bacon rashers that have been dry cured.

Serves 4

1 ciabatta loaf
olive oil, for cooking
20 rindless pancetta slices (Italian streaky bacon)
4 large eggs
4 teaspoons tomato ketchup
4 teaspoons wholegrain mustard (preferably Dalkey)
salt and freshly ground black pepper

Heat a large frying pan and preheat the grill. Cut the ciabatta loaf in half lengthways, then in half widthways to give four pieces. Arrange on a grill rack and lightly toast for a couple of minutes, then drizzle a little olive oil over each one and keep warm.

Add 1 teaspoon of the oil to the heated frying pan and fry the pancetta for 1–2 minutes on each side, until crisp and golden brown. Put onto a baking sheet and keep warm. Wipe out the frying pan and add a thin layer of olive oil. Break in the eggs, season to taste and then gently fry for a couple of minutes, spooning a little of the hot oil over the yolks, until they are just set.

To serve, arrange the ciabatta on warmed plates and spread over the tomato ketchup and mustard. Top each one with a fried egg and then pile the crispy pancetta on top.

Sausage and red onion soda farls

Very simple, very tasty and very more-ish. I like to use Moyallon sausages from their black spot rare-breed pigs reared in County Down. They are widely available, especially in farmers' markets up and down the country, so keep an eye out for them. Alternatively, try to buy from a craft butcher; the flavour will always be so much better.

Serves 4

8 pork and leek sausages
1 red onion, thinly sliced
olive oil, for drizzling
4 soda farls
1–2 teaspoons Dijon mustard
salt and freshly ground black pepper

For the tomato chutney
1 tablespoon olive oil
2 ripe vine tomatoes, finely chopped
1 shallot, finely chopped
1 tablespoon balsamic vinegar
large pinch light muscovado sugar
½ teaspoon chopped fresh thyme

To make the tomato chutney, heat the olive oil in a pan. Add the tomatoes, shallot, balsamic vinegar, sugar and thyme and simmer gently for 10–15 minutes, until the tomatoes have softened and the chutney is slightly reduced. Remove from the heat and leave to cool completely, then transfer to a bowl and store in the fridge covered with cling film until needed.

Preheat a flat griddle or large frying pan until hot. Add the sausages and cook for 8–10 minutes, until golden brown and cooked through, turning occasionally. Drain on kitchen paper and keep warm.

Add the red onion to the pan, season to taste and drizzle over a little olive oil, then cook for about for 4 minutes, until softened and lightly golden, stirring occasionally.

LIMERICK
COUNTY LIBRARY
00667399

Split the soda farls open at one end to make pockets. Cut the sausages in half and put them into the farls with the sautéed red onion. Drizzle some mustard and tomato chutney over the sausages and press the edges together. Toast the farls on the griddle for 1 ½ minutes on each side, until heated through and lightly toasted. Cut each farl on the diagonal and arrange on warmed plates to serve.

Mozzarella and tomato bagel melt

Mozzarella and tomato go together like ham and eggs or fish and chips – natural partners of the food world. To make this dish sing, you must use the best-quality ingredients available. Of course, you could add some grilled crispy bacon or smoked salmon, but I love it just the way it is.

Serves 4

4 plain bagels
150 g (5 oz) ball mozzarella cheese, sliced
2 large ripe vine tomatoes, sliced
8 fresh basil leaves
olive oil, for drizzling
Maldon sea salt and freshly ground black pepper

Preheat the oven to 190°C/375°F/gas 5. Split the bagels in half horizontally, arrange the mozzarella slices on the bagel bases, then lay the tomato slices on top.

Tear the basil leaves and scatter over the tomatoes, then drizzle each one with olive oil. Season generously and cover with the bagel tops. Press down lightly.

Arrange the filled bagels on a baking sheet and bake for 10–15 minutes, until the cheese has melted and the bagels are crisp and lightly golden. Cut each bagel in half and arrange on warmed plates to serve.

Banana cinnamon pancakes

If you want to make these pancakes before serving them up, stack them with a square of greaseproof paper between each one. They will sit happily like this for a couple of hours. The batter benefits from resting for at least half an hour but would be fine for a couple of days in the fridge if covered with cling film.

Serves 4–6

125 g (4 ½ oz) plain flour
½ teaspoon ground cinnamon
pinch of salt
1 egg
300 ml (½ pint) milk
sunflower oil, for frying
4 large bananas
about 4 teaspoons runny honey or maple syrup
2–4 tablespoons vanilla yoghurt
icing sugar, to dust

Sift the flour, cinnamon and salt into a bowl, make a well in the centre and crack in the egg. Using a balloon whisk, gradually beat in the milk to make a smooth batter. If you have time, leave to rest in the fridge for 30 minutes.

Heat a non-stick frying pan. Once hot but not smoking, add a few drops of sunflower oil and then ladle in some batter, quickly swirling to cover the bottom of the pan in a thin layer. Cook for a minute or so on each side, then slide onto a plate and keep warm. Repeat with the remaining batter to make at least 12 pancakes.

Meanwhile, peel and slice bananas. Place the pancakes on warm plates and fold over into triangles, slightly overlapping. Scatter over sliced bananas and then drizzle with the honey or maple syrup. Add a dollop of yoghurt to each one and sprinkle a light dusting of icing sugar on top to serve.

Red berry smoothie

This breakfast in a glass is the perfect way to start the day. If the fruit is nice and ripe, there's no need to sweeten with sugar or honey, but that, of course, is personal preference. I normally use frozen berries straight out of the freezer so that you don't have to use any ice cubes, which can be hard on the blades of your liquidiser. They are just as nutritious as fresh berries and normally half the price.

Serves 4

225 g (8 oz) frozen berries, such as a mixture of strawberries,
raspberries, redcurrants and tayberries
275 g (10 oz) natural yoghurt (preferably organic)
600 ml (1 pint) semi-skimmed milk
handful of ice cubes
fresh mint sprigs, to decorate

Place the berries in a liquidiser with the yoghurt and milk. Process for 1 minute, until smooth. Alternatively, you can put everything into a large measuring jug and blend with a hand-held blender, moving it up and down, until smooth.

Half-fill tall glasses with ice cubes and pour in the red berry smoothie. Decorate with a mint sprig to serve.

Variations

Mango lassi

Place the diced flesh from two ripe mangoes into the liquidiser with 275 g (10 oz) natural yoghurt and 300 ml (½ pint) of freshly pressed apple juice. Blend until smooth and pour into tall glasses half-filled with ice cubes. Serve at once.

Strawberry booster

Place 225 g (8 oz) of frozen strawberries into the food processor with 2 table-spoons of runny honey, 1 tablespoon of wheat germ, if liked, 450 g (1 lb) of natural yoghurt and 225 ml (8 fl oz) of semi-skimmed milk. Blend until smooth and pour into tall glasses half-filled with ice cubes.

Jungle boogie

Tropical and healthy – I like to use a wide straw to suck up all that goodness. It's such a good pick-me-up in the morning that a jug never hangs around very long. Get the children to muck in and help put everything in the liquidiser, then, under careful supervision, let them switch the machine on!

Serves 4

1 large mango, peeled, stone removed and chopped
½ fresh pineapple, peeled, core removed and chopped
4 ripe nectarines, halved, stoned and chopped
300 ml (½ pint) fresh orange and passion fruit juice
about 175 g (6 oz) ice cubes

Place the mango in a liquidiser with the pineapple, nectarine and fruit juice. Alternatively, you can put everything into a large measuring jug and blend with a handheld blender, moving it up and down, until smooth.

Blend until smooth and pour into tall glasses filled with ice cubes. Add a thick straw to each one to serve, if liked.

Variations

Raspberry passion

Place 225 g (8 oz) of fresh or frozen raspberries into a liquidiser with the juice of 2 limes, 400 ml (14 fl oz) of passion fruit juice and 400 ml (14 fl oz) of cranberry juice. Blend until smooth and pour into tall glasses filled with ice cubes.

Green-flecked frenzy

Rip a bunch of mint leaves into a liquidiser and add 4 peeled and chopped kiwi fruit with 2 chopped ripe bananas and 600 ml (1 pint) of grapefruit juice. Blend until smooth and pour into tall glasses filled with ice cubes.

Soups
and lunches

Roasted red pepper soup

Chargrilled peppers have the most wonderful, smoky sweetness, which I just adore. Collect as much of the juice as possible as you peel them, as it really has a great flavour.

Serves 4–6

6 red peppers, halved, cored and seeded
5 tablespoons olive oil
1 tablespoon balsamic vinegar
½ teaspoon chopped fresh thyme
2 onions, finely chopped
2 garlic cloves, crushed
2 tablespoons tomato purée
1.2 litres (2 pints) chicken or vegetable stock
2 tablespoons torn fresh basil
Maldon sea salt and freshly ground black pepper
basil oil or pesto, to garnish
freshly baked ciabatta, to serve (optional)

Preheat the oven to 190°C/375°F/gas 5. Arrange the pepper halves in a baking tin, cut side up. Drizzle over 4 tablespoons of the olive oil, then sprinkle the vinegar, thyme and 1 teaspoon of the salt on top. Place in the oven and roast for 20 minutes, until softened and lightly golden.

When the peppers are cool enough to handle, slip the skins off the peppers and discard, then roughly chop the flesh, reserving as much of the juice as possible. Set aside until needed.

Heat the remaining tablespoon of oil in a pan, add the onions and garlic and sweat for 10 minutes until lightly golden, stirring occasionally. Add the reserved pepper flesh with the tomato purée and stock and bring to the boil. Reduce the heat and simmer for 10–15 minutes, until slightly reduced. Add the basil and then blitz with a hand blender until smooth. Season to taste.

Ladle the soup into warmed bowls and drizzle with a little basil oil or pesto, then serve with some ciabatta bread.

Butternut squash soup with cheese toasties

I love all soups made with winter squashes, but this one has a wonderful, subtle, almost nutty flavour that is hard to beat, especially when it's served with toasted cheese sandwiches. For a smoother, more velvety finish, pass the soup through a fine sieve.

Serves 4–6

RTÊ **GUIDE**

READER TESTED

2 tablespoons olive oil
2 onions, chopped
2 garlic cloves, finely chopped
1 kg (2 ¼ lb) butternut squash, peeled, seeded and cubed
1.2 litres (2 pints) vegetable or chicken stock
4 fresh thyme sprigs
200 g (7 oz) crème fraîche

For the cheese toasties

50 g (2 oz) butter
8 slices white bread
200 g (7 oz) Gruyère cheese, grated

1 tablespoon snipped fresh chives
salt and freshly ground black pepper

Heat the oil in a large pan. Cook the onions, garlic and butternut squash over a gentle heat for 10 minutes, until the onions have softened but not coloured, stirring occasionally. Pour in the stock and add the thyme. Bring to the boil, then reduce the heat, cover and simmer for about 25 minutes, until the butternut squash is tender.

To make the cheese toasties, butter the bread and arrange the cheese over half of the slices, buttered side down. Sprinkle over the chives and cover with the remaining slices, buttered side up.

Preheat a griddle or large non-stick frying pan and cook the sandwiches two at a time for 2 minutes on each side, until golden brown and the cheese has melted. Cut into fingers and keep hot.

Remove the thyme stalks from the soup, then purée with a hand blender until smooth. Stir in the crème fraîche and reheat gently. Season to taste.

Serve in a warm bowl with the cheese toasties stacked on the side.

Roasted root vegetable soup

You can substitute pumpkin, turnip or celeriac for the swede, or just use a mixture – this is a very flexible recipe. You don't have to add the cream if you're watching the calories, but you might need a little extra stock to thin the soup a little.

Serves 4–6

1 small swede, cut into cubes
2 carrots, cut into cubes
1 parsnip, cut into cubes
3 tablespoons olive oil
1 onion, finely chopped
2 celery stalks, finely chopped
1 garlic clove, crushed
1 teaspoon chopped fresh thyme
1.2 litres (2 pints) vegetable or chicken stock
150 ml (¼ pint) single cream
salt and freshly ground black pepper

Preheat the oven to 200°C/400°F/gas 6. Place the swede, carrots and parsnip into a roasting tin and drizzle over 2 tablespoons of the olive oil. Season generously and roast for 25–30 minutes, until golden brown and tender, shaking the tin occasionally to ensure even cooking.

Meanwhile, heat the remaining tablespoon of olive oil in a large heavy-based pan and add the onion, celery, garlic and thyme. Stir well to combine and then fry for 4–5 minutes, until softened but not browned, stirring occasionally.

Add the roasted root vegetables to the pan and then pour in the stock. Bring gently to the boil, then reduce the heat, cover and simmer for 25–30 minutes, until completely tender, stirring occasionally. Purée with a hand blender until completely smooth.

To serve, stir the cream into the soup. Gently heat through and season to taste, then ladle into warmed bowls.

Chinese-style chicken and sweetcorn soup

This is my version on an old favourite that appears on every Chinese takeaway menu in the country. I really like the fresh flavours in this version. It makes a truly satisfying meal in a bowl.

Serves 4–6

1 tablespoon sunflower oil
2 garlic cloves, crushed
1 teaspoon freshly grated root ginger
2 skinless chicken breast fillets, finely sliced
1 tablespoon mild curry paste
1 heaped teaspoon cornflour
1.2 litres (2 pints) chicken stock
275 g (10 oz) can sweetcorn kernels, drained
1 tablespoon sweet chilli sauce
1 tablespoon dark soy sauce
1 teaspoon toasted sesame oil
salt and freshly ground black pepper

Heat the sunflower oil in a large pan. Add the garlic, ginger and chicken and stir-fry for 3 minutes, until sealed, then stir in the curry paste and cook for 1 minute, stirring.

Mix the cornflour with a little stock, then add to the pan with the remaining stock, stirring until smooth. Add the sweetcorn with the sweet chilli and soy sauce, then bring to the boil, stirring constantly. Simmer gently for 5 minutes, until heated through and slightly thickened. Season to taste.

To serve, ladle the soup into warmed bowls and trickle a few drops of the sesame oil over each one.

New England smoked haddock chowder

This is an American version of the well-known Cullen skink, a rich soup from the Moray Firth, the home of Finnan haddock. Avoid any smoked haddock that has been dyed bright yellow, as the flavour is normally disappointing.

Serves 4–6

25 g (1 oz) butter
1 small onion, diced
2 tablespoons diced leek
1 small carrot, diced
50 g (2 oz) smoked bacon, rind removed and diced (dry cured, if possible)
25 g (1 oz) fresh thyme, leaves stripped and finely chopped
300 ml (½ pint) dry white wine
600 ml (1 pint) light chicken or fish stock
900 g (2 lb) natural smoked haddock fillets, pin bones removed
2 large potatoes, diced
2 teaspoons cornflour
300 ml (½ pint) double cream
1 tablespoon chopped fresh flat-leaf parsley
salt and freshly ground black pepper

Heat a heavy-based pan. Melt the butter and add the onion, leek, carrot, bacon and thyme. Cook for 10 minutes until softened but not coloured, stirring occasionally. Pour in the wine and allow to bubble down, then pour over the stock and bring to a gentle simmer.

Add the haddock fillets to the simmering stock mixture and cook gently for about 5 minutes, until just tender, then lift out with a fish slice and place on a plate. Roughly flake the flesh, discarding any skin and stray bones. Set aside.

Add the potatoes to the stock mixture and simmer for another 8–10 minutes, until tender. Blend the cornflour in a small bowl with a little water and then stir into the soup. Simmer for 1 minute, until thickened, then stir in the cream. Add the parsley and reserved haddock, then season to taste. Allow to warm through, stirring occasionally.

To serve, ladle the chowder into warmed bowls.

Sweet potato soup with ginger and coconut

Coconut milk, one of my favourite ingredients, makes a fantastic creamy base for all the other robust flavours in this Asian-style soup. Choose firm sweet potatoes with orange flesh for their vibrant colour.

Serves 4–6

450 g (1 lb) sweet potatoes, peeled and cut into cubes
2 tablespoons sunflower oil
1 onion, finely chopped
1 leek, finely chopped
1 teaspoon freshly grated root ginger
½ red chilli, seeded and finely chopped
1 lemon grass stalk, trimmed and halved
1.2 litres (2 pints) chicken or vegetable stock
1 tablespoon tomato purée
250 ml (9 fl oz) coconut milk
2 tablespoons torn fresh basil
salt and freshly ground black pepper

Preheat the oven to 200°C/400°F/gas 6. Place the sweet potatoes in a baking tin, drizzle over half the sunflower oil, tossing to coat evenly, and roast for 20–30 minutes, until tender. Set aside.

Heat the remaining oil in a pan. Add the onion, leek, ginger, chilli and lemon grass and sweat for 4 minutes, stirring occasionally. Add the reserved roasted sweet potatoes with the stock and tomato purée, then bring to the boil. Reduce the heat and simmer for 10 minutes or until the liquid has slightly reduced and all of the vegetables are completely tender, stirring occasionally.

Pour the coconut milk into the pan and cook for another 5 minutes, stirring constantly. Season to taste. Remove the lemon grass and then blend with a hand blender until smooth.

To serve, ladle the soup into warmed bowls and scatter over the basil.

Prawn and avocado roll

*This is an updated version of the classic prawn mayonnaise sandwich,
which is still one of the most popular shop-bought sandwiches. To change
the filling, try using leftover roasted vegetables with feta or roast beef
with a smear of onion marmalade and plenty of rocket.*

Serves 4

1 large, ripe avocado
a good dash of balsamic vinegar
squeeze of fresh lemon juice
2 tablespoons mayonnaise
4 soft flour tortillas
50 g (2 oz) wild rocket
350 g (12 oz) large cooked, peeled prawns
salt and freshly ground black pepper

Heat a heavy-based frying pan. Cut the avocado in half and remove the stone,
then scoop the flesh out into a bowl and add the balsamic vinegar, lemon juice
and the mayonnaise. Season to taste and mash with a fork to a smooth purée.
Heat each flour tortilla for 30 seconds on the frying pan, turning once.

Spoon the avocado mash down the middle of each of the heated tortillas and
stack the rocket and prawns on top. Season to taste and roll up to enclose
the filling.

To serve, cut each one on the diagonal and arrange on plates or wrap in
greaseproof paper to pack for lunch boxes.

Sticky lemon chicken wings

These baked chicken wings are so easy to make and taste absolutely delicious. I love them hot from the oven, but they are also fantastic cold the next day, packed into a lunchbox or picnic basket.

Serves 4–6

12 large chicken wings
25 g (1 oz) butter
finely grated rind and juice of 1 lemon
2 tablespoons dark soy sauce
1 tablespoon clear honey
2 tablespoons sweet chilli sauce
salt and freshly ground black pepper

Preheat the oven to 200°C/400°F/gas 6. Using a strong pair of scissors, snip the tip off each wing and discard.

Melt the butter in a bowl in the microwave or in a small pan. Stir in the lemon rind and juice with the soy sauce, honey and chilli sauce. Season to taste.

Arrange the chicken wings on a rack set over a baking tin and brush both sides of the wings with the mixture. Roast for 30–40 minutes, turning and basting once or twice with the remaining lemon mixture, until golden brown.

To serve, arrange on a large platter straight from the oven or leave to cool and then chill in rigid plastic containers to take on a picnic or in a packed lunch.

Chicken tikka wraps

Soft flour tortillas offer a healthy but tasty alternative to traditional breads.
Alternatively, substitute pitta bread, which is just as transportable. If I was
serving this at home, I'd slice it on the diagonal and serve each one with a
wedge of lemon.

Serves 4

150 g (5 oz) natural yoghurt
1 garlic clove, crushed
1 teaspoon ground cumin
½ teaspoon cayenne pepper
½ teaspoon ground turmeric
4 small skinless chicken breast fillets
4 soft flour tortilla wraps
4 large iceberg lettuce leaves, shredded
salt and freshly ground black pepper
lemon wedges, to garnish (optional)

Preheat the grill. Place the yoghurt in a bowl and add the garlic, cumin, cayenne
pepper and turmeric. Season to taste and mix until well combined. Cut the
chicken breast fillets into thin strips and stir into the yoghurt mixture. Cover with
cling film and set aside to marinate in the fridge for up to 24 hours if time allows.

Arrange the yoghurt-coated chicken strips on a foil-lined grill rack and cook for
about 6 minutes, turning occasionally, until cooked through and lightly golden.

Meanwhile, warm the tortilla wraps in the microwave or on a dry heated frying
pan for about 15 seconds on each side. Divide the chicken tikka among the
warmed tortilla wraps and scatter with shredded lettuce.

To serve, roll up tightly, then wrap in greaseproof paper to pack for lunch boxes
or cut on the diagonal and arrange on plates and garnish with the lemon
wedges.

Little palm bacon and chicken pies

This is a novel way of using a muffin tin to make dinky little pies that will fit into the palm of your hand. They freeze brilliantly and just need to be defrosted at room temperature for 2 hours. Alternatively, make them up to 1 day in advance and then bake them on the day.

Makes 12

1 tablespoon sunflower oil
100 g (4 oz) rindless smoked streaky bacon, cut into small strips
2 skinless chicken breast fillets
1 teaspoon cornflour
1 onion, finely chopped
1 teaspoon chopped fresh sage
100 ml (3 ½ fl oz) chicken stock
squeeze of lemon juice
450 g (1 lb) ready-made shortcrust pastry, thawed if frozen
1 egg yolk
salt and freshly ground black pepper

Heat a large non-stick frying pan and add the oil. Cook the bacon for 3–4 minutes, until crisp and golden brown. Remove with a slotted spoon and set aside.

Cut the chicken breasts into small cubes and dust with the cornflour. Add to the frying pan with the onion and cook for 8–10 minutes, until well browned and cooked through. Add the sage, then stir in the stock and bring to the boil. Reduce the heat and simmer for 1–2 minutes, until slightly thickened. Add a squeeze of lemon juice and stir in the cooked bacon. Season to taste and leave to cool.

Preheat the oven to 200°C/400°F/gas 6. Roll out three-quarters of the pastry and cut into 12 cm x 7 ½ cm (6 inch) discs. Use to line a 12-hole muffin tin, allowing the excess pastry to hang over the edges. Roll out the remaining pastry and cut 12 cm x 7 ½ cm (3 inch) discs for lids.

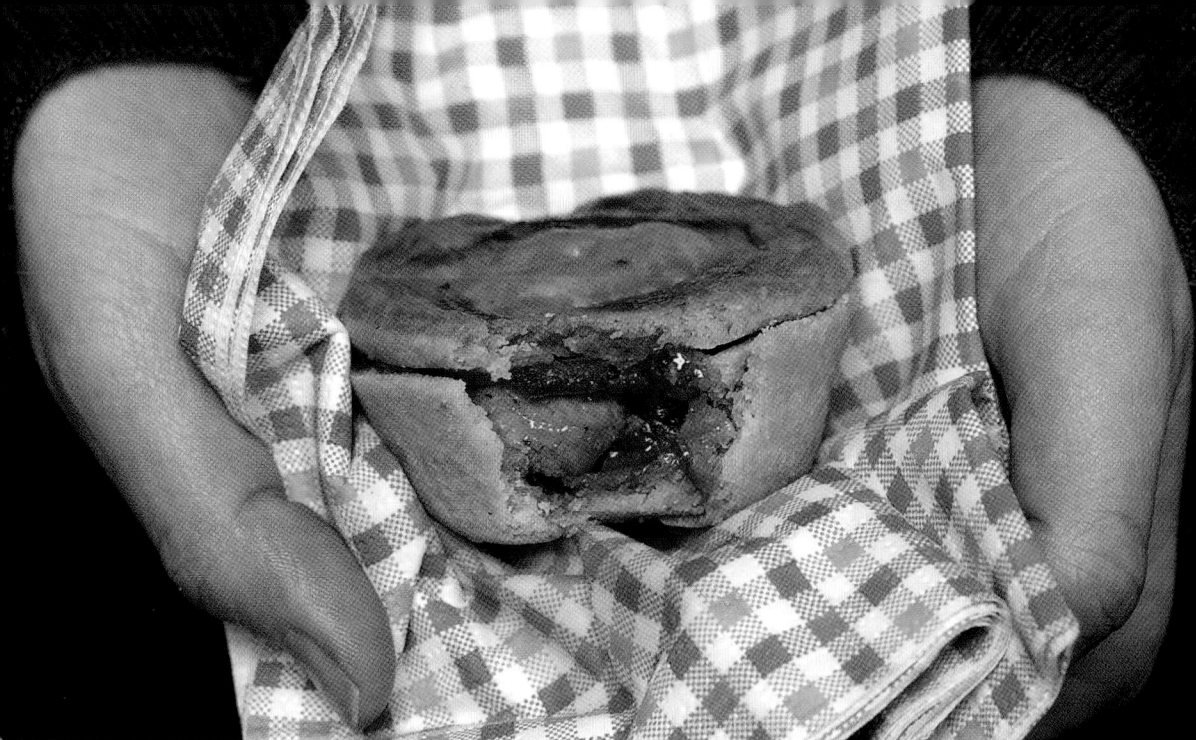

Divide the bacon and chicken mixture among the pastry cases, then brush the inside edges with a little water. Lay the pastry lids on top of the filling, then fold the edges of the pastry over and press together to seal. Cut a small hole on top of each pie.

Mix the egg yolk in a small bowl with a pinch of salt and brush over the pies, then bake for 25–30 minutes, until the pastry is crisp and well glazed.

To serve, arrange on plates warm from the oven or leave to cool, then wrap individually in greaseproof paper to pack for lunch boxes.

Sesame chicken noodle salad

This salad is a fantastic way to use up leftover roast chicken and just the thing for an exotic transportable feast. For a change, omit the red pepper and add one finely diced peeled mango instead.

Serves 4–6

350 g (12 oz) flat or vermicelli rice noodles
350 g (12 oz) cooked chicken breast
2 tablespoons light soy sauce
4 tablespoons sweet chilli sauce
1 small red pepper, cored, seeded and thinly sliced
1 bunch spring onions, trimmed and finely sliced
2 tablespoons toasted sesame seeds
2 teaspoons toasted sesame oil
handful fresh coriander leaves, torn
4 tablespoons salted peanuts, roughly chopped (optional)
salt and freshly ground black pepper

Place the rice noodles in a heatproof bowl. Pour over enough boiling water to cover completely and leave to soak for 5 minutes or according to packet instructions.

Meanwhile, remove skin from the chicken and discard, then cut the flesh into fine strips. Place in a bowl and add the soy and sweet chilli sauce. Toss well to combine.

Drain the rice noodles, then refresh under cold water and drain thoroughly. Add the chicken strips with the red pepper, spring onions, sesame seeds and sesame oil. Toss well and season to taste. Add the torn coriander leaves and scatter over the peanuts, if using.

To serve, arrange on plates or divide among plastic tubs for lunch boxes.

Chunky hummus, roasted red pepper and spinach pitta

Hummus is a traditional Middle Eastern dip made from chickpeas and tahini, which is a sesame seed pulp. I've substituted sesame oil for tahini, as I normally have some in the cupboard, but you can leave it out altogether if you like.

Serves 4

2 garlic cloves, roughly chopped
1 mild red chilli, seeded and roughly chopped
handful fresh flat-leaf parsley leaves
400 g (14 oz) can chickpeas, drained and rinsed
2 tablespoons extra virgin olive oil
1 tablespoon toasted sesame oil (optional)
4 white pitta breads
50 g (2 oz) young tender spinach leaves
400 g (14 oz) can or jar roasted red peppers, drained and sliced
salt and freshly ground black pepper

Place the garlic, chilli and parsley in a food processor and whizz until finely chopped. Add half of the chickpeas with the olive oil and the sesame oil, if using, then whizz again until smooth. Add the remaining chickpeas and pulse for another 10 seconds, until just combined so that the hummus still has plenty of texture.

Preheat the grill or a griddle pan and quickly toast the pitta breads on both sides. Split open and stuff with the chunky hummus, spinach and roasted red peppers.

To serve, wrap the filled pittas in greaseproof paper to pack for lunch boxes or cut on the diagonal and arrange on plates.

The ultimate tuna mayonnaise

This all-time favourite is the perfect store cupboard standby. You could replace the spring onions with a couple of tablespoons of diced red or white onion, or even chives work well.

Serves 4

4 poppy seed bagels, split
6 tablespoons mayonnaise
4 spring onions, finely chopped
2 tablespoons capers, rinsed
1 teaspoon Dijon mustard
1 teaspoon freshly grated horseradish (or from a jar is fine)
squeeze of fresh lemon juice
400 g (14 oz) can tuna in oil, drained
salt and freshly ground black pepper

Preheat the grill and lightly toast the bagels, cut side up.

Meanwhile, place the mayonnaise in a bowl and beat in the spring onions, capers, mustard, horseradish and a squeeze of lemon juice. Season to taste and gently fold in the tuna.

Divide the tuna mayonnaise among the bottom halves of the bagels, then sandwich together and cut each one in half.

To serve, wrap in greaseproof paper and place in lunch boxes or arrange on plates.

Everyday
suppers

Spaghetti with prawns and mussels

Experiment by using clams instead of the mussels, or a mixture also works well. If your pasta starts to stick once it's cooked, toss with a splash of olive oil. For a healthier version, omit the cream and use 150 ml (¼ pint) of fish or vegetable stock instead.

Serves 4–6

350 g (12 oz) spaghetti
150 ml (¼ pint) dry white wine
2 garlic cloves, crushed
1 red chilli, seeded and finely chopped
300 ml (½ pint) cream
900 g (2 lb) fresh mussels, cleaned
450 g (1 lb) cooked peeled tiger prawns
1 tablespoon shredded fresh basil
1 tablespoon chopped fresh flat-leaf parsley
a little extra virgin olive oil
salt and freshly ground black pepper
lemon wedges, to garnish
crusty bread, to serve

Cook the spaghetti in a large pan of boiling salted water for 8–10 minutes, or as per packet instructions, until al dente (tender but still firm to the bite).

Meanwhile, pour the wine into a separate large pan and add the garlic, chilli and cream. Bring to the boil, then reduce the heat and simmer for 5 minutes.

Add the mussels to the pan, cover tightly and cook for 3–4 minutes, shaking the pan halfway through. All the mussels should have now opened – discard any that have not.

Drain the pasta and tip into the pan with the mussel mixture, then add the tiger prawns, basil and parsley. Stir gently until well combined and season to taste.

To serve, divide the spaghetti with the prawns and mussels among warmed bowls and drizzle a little olive oil over each one. Garnish with lemon wedges and serve with a separate bowl of crusty bread.

Butter-roasted haddock with spring onion mash

Flavour the fish with a sprinkling of finely chopped fresh chilli or lemon grass or a smear of chilli sauce, if you like. The potatoes can be mashed with a little warm milk and a knob of butter if you prefer a creamier mash.

Serves 6

1.75 kg (4 lb) floury potatoes
50 g (2 oz) butter
4–6 x 150 g (5 oz) skinless haddock fillets, boned
finely grated rind of 2 limes
1 tablespoon chopped fresh flat-leaf parsley
1 bunch spring onions, trimmed and thinly sliced
4 tablespoons olive oil
salt and freshly ground black pepper

Preheat the oven to 220°C/425°F/gas 7. Cook the potatoes in a large pan of boiling salted water for 15–20 minutes, until tender.

Cut 4 to 6 rectangles of parchment paper large enough to sit a piece of fish on. Lightly butter each piece of paper and place on a baking sheet. Put the haddock on the paper and smear with the remaining butter, then sprinkle over the lime rind and flat-leaf parsley. Season to taste.

When the potatoes are almost cooked, pop the fish into the oven and roast for 6–8 minutes, until just tender – this will depend on the thickness of the fillets. Drain the potatoes and return to the pan. Mash well and then beat in the spring onions and olive oil. Season to taste.

To serve, divide the spring onion mash among warmed plates. Gently ease each piece of fish off the paper on top of the mash.

Stir-fry chilli steak with tortilla chips

This stir-fry is a wonderful combination of flavours and textures that is incredibly simple to prepare. I like to serve it as part of a help-yourself feast with home-made guacamole (see page 116), plain boiled rice, sour cream and tortilla chips.

Serves 4–6

1 tablespoon sunflower oil
500 g (1 lb 2 oz) rump steak, cut into thin strips
1 red onion, thinly sliced
1 red pepper, cored, seeded and thinly sliced
1 red chilli, seeded and thinly sliced
1 teaspoon cumin seeds (optional)
1 teaspoon cayenne pepper
400 g (14 oz) can chopped tomatoes
400 g (14 oz) can cannellini beans, drained and rinsed
3 tablespoons sweet chilli sauce
1 tablespoon chopped fresh flat-leaf parsley
300 ml (½ pint) sour cream
175 g (6 oz) tortilla chips
salt and freshly ground black pepper
plain boiled rice and guacamole (shop-bought or home-made – see recipe on page 116), to serve

Heat a wok until very hot. Add the oil, swirling it up the sides. Tip in the steak and stir-fry for 3 minutes, until sealed and just starting to brown. Add the onion and red pepper, then sprinkle over the red chilli, cumin seeds (if using) and cayenne pepper. Stir-fry for 2 minutes.

Stir in the tomatoes and cook for another couple of minutes. Add the cannellini beans and chilli sauce, then simmer for 5 minutes, until piping hot. Season to taste and stir in the parsley.

To serve, spoon a mound of rice onto each warmed plate and make a dent in the middle. Add the stir-fry chilli steak and pass around bowls of the sour cream, tortilla chips and guacamole.

Spiced chicken and herb couscous

Simple but stylish. This dish is perfect for eating al fresco, whether you decide to cook it under the grill or on a barbecue. Use pork fillets or sirloin steak instead of the chicken if you prefer.

Serves 4–6

RTÉ **GUIDE**

READER TESTED

4–6 chicken breast supremes (wings still attached)
2–3 teaspoons harissa, chilli paste or sweet chilli sauce
300 g (11 oz) couscous
1 red onion, finely diced
350 ml (12 fl oz) chicken stock
grated rind and juice of 1 lemon
3 tablespoons olive oil
150 g (5 oz) cherry tomatoes, halved
200 g (7 oz) feta cheese, crumbled into small pieces
4 tablespoons chopped fresh flat-leaf parsley
4 tablespoons chopped fresh coriander
salt and freshly ground black pepper
lime wedges, to garnish

Preheat the oven to 160°C/325°F/gas 3 and preheat the grill to medium. Slash the skin side of the chicken, then rub the harissa or chilli paste or sweet chilli sauce into each chicken breast, making sure it goes deep into the slashes. Season to taste.

Place the chicken skin side up on a foil-lined grill pan. Cook for 8–10 minutes on each side or until chicken is cooked through and the skin is crisp.

Meanwhile, place the couscous and red onion in a roasting tin and cook for 5 minutes, until the couscous is lightly toasted and the onion has begun to crisp, stirring once or twice to ensure that it cooks evenly.

Heat the stock in a small pan or in the microwave. Place the toasted couscous and onion into a pan and pour over the hot stock, then stir in the lemon juice and 2 tablespoons of the olive oil. Cover and leave to soak for 5 minutes, until all the liquid has been absorbed.

Place the couscous on the hob and heat gently for 2–3 minutes while breaking up the grains with a fork. Remove from the heat and fold in the remaining olive oil with the lemon rind, tomatoes, feta, parsley and coriander. Season to taste.

To serve, arrange the herb couscous on warm plates with the chicken and garnish each one with lime wedges.

Lamb koftas with tzatziki

These kebabs are an excellent dish to serve to the whole family or a gang of hungry teenagers. As everything gets cooked under the grill, there's the added bonus of very little washing up to do afterwards.

Serves 4

500 g (1 lb 2 oz) lean minced lamb
1 small onion, finely chopped
1 teaspoon chopped fresh oregano
1 teaspoon ground coriander
3 tablespoons chopped fresh flat-leaf parsley
½ small cucumber
150 g (5 oz) natural yoghurt
1 garlic clove, crushed
4 pitta breads
good handful salad leaves, such as baby spinach, rocket and/or watercress
salt and freshly ground black pepper
lemon wedges, to garnish

Preheat the grill to high. Soak 8 x 20 cm (8 inch) bamboo skewers in hot water for 10 minutes.

Mix the lamb with the onion, oregano, coriander and 2 tablespoons of the parsley. Season to taste and mix well to combine. Divide into 24 portions and then shape each piece into a cylinder that is 6 cm (2 ½ inches) long and 2 ½ cm (1 inch) wide. Thread three onto each of the pre-soaked skewers.

Arrange the lamb kebabs on a grill pan and cook for 10 minutes, turning occasionally, until well browned and cooked through.

To make the tzatziki, grate the cucumber and, using your hands, squeeze out the excess liquid. Place in a bowl, then stir in the yoghurt and garlic with the rest of the parsley. Season to taste.

Warm the pitta breads under the grill, turning once, then chop into pieces.

To serve, arrange the lamb kebabs on warmed plates with the pitta. Add a small mound of salad leaves to each one with a good dollop of the tzatziki to the side. Garnish with lemon wedges.

Pork chops with rosemary and mushrooms baked in foil

Individual parcels can be made and served unopened to your guests. However, I find that making just a family-sized one is the handiest and gives excellent results. Serve with some plain boiled rice for a healthier option than the mashed potatoes.

Serves 4–6

1 tablespoon olive oil
4–6 lean pork chops (preferably saddleback), well trimmed of excess fat
knob of butter
1 red onion, thinly sliced
275 g (10 oz) chestnut mushrooms, sliced
4 tablespoons crème fraîche
1 garlic clove, crushed
1 teaspoon Dijon mustard
1 tablespoon chopped fresh flat-leaf parsley
good pinch chopped fresh rosemary (optional)
salt and freshly ground black pepper
mashed potatoes and sautéed spinach, to serve (optional)

Preheat the oven to 180°C/350°F/gas 5. Take a large piece of foil, fold in half and place on a baking sheet. Heat the olive oil in a pan and quickly sear the chops on both sides until golden brown. Place side by side on the folded foil.

Melt the butter in the pan, stir in the onion and mushrooms, then sauté for a few minutes, until tender, and season to taste. Scatter over the pork chops. Mix the crème fraîche in a small bowl with the garlic, Dijon mustard, parsley and rosemary, if using, then drizzle over the chops.

Seal the edges of the foil together with a double fold, making sure that there will be plenty of room for expansion. Bake for 30 minutes, until the parcel has puffed up and the pork chops are completely tender inside.

To serve, open the parcel at the table for that special effect and serve the pork chops on warmed plates, spooning over all the lovely juices. Add some mashed potatoes and sautéed spinach, if liked.

Chorizo and spinach pasta

This pasta dish is easy to make and perfect for a cold winter night. The sauce can be made the day before, as chorizo seems to taste even better the next day and makes a nice change from your average tomato-flavoured sauce. Experiment with other gourmet flavoured sausages.

Serves 6

450 g (1 lb) chorizo sausage, cut into 2 ½ cm (1 inch) pieces on the diagonal
2 onions, thinly sliced
3 garlic cloves, crushed
1 red chilli, seeded and finely chopped
2 tablespoons shredded fresh basil
2 x 400 g (14 oz) cans chopped tomatoes
1 teaspoon light muscovado sugar
500 g (1 lb 2 oz) penne pasta
100 g (4 oz) baby spinach leaves
salt and freshly ground black pepper
freshly grated Parmesan, to serve

Heat a sauté pan and tip in the chorizo sausage pieces, then cook for 2 minutes, tossing the pan occasionally to ensure they cook evenly. Add the onions and garlic, then cook for another 5 minutes, until the onions are golden, stirring occasionally.

Stir the chilli into the chorizo and onion mixture with the basil and cook for 1 minute. Pour in the tomatoes, add the sugar and season to taste. Bring to the boil, then reduce the heat and simmer for 30 minutes, until slightly reduced and thickened, stirring occasionally.

Meanwhile, cook the pasta in a large pan of boiling salted water for 8–10 minutes or according to the packet instructions, until al dente (tender but still firm to the bite). Drain well and return to the pan. Stir in the sausage sauce with the spinach and mix well to combine – the heat of the pasta and sauce should cook the spinach instantly.

To serve, divide the chorizo and spinach pasta among warmed bowls and scatter over the freshly grated Parmesan, then add a good grinding of pepper.

Aromatic fish cakes with lemon mayonnaise

I normally have some smoked haddock in the freezer, but these fish cakes also work well with salmon or cod. They are a great way to get children to eat fish, but they might like the lemon mayonnaise more with a dash of tomato ketchup!

Serves 4–6

1 kg (2 ¼ lb) floury potatoes, diced
400 g (14 oz) natural smoked haddock fillets
300 ml (½ pint) milk
1 teaspoon mild curry paste
1 bunch spring onions, trimmed and thinly sliced
1 tablespoon chopped fresh coriander
1 tablespoon chopped fresh flat-leaf parsley
4 tablespoons plain flour
2 eggs, beaten
100 g (4 oz) fresh white breadcrumbs
1 tablespoon sesame seeds
4 tablespoons sunflower oil
6 tablespoons mayonnaise
squeeze of lemon juice
2 tablespoons snipped fresh chives
salt and freshly ground black pepper
mixed salad leaves, to serve
lime wedges, to garnish

Boil the potatoes in a large pan of boiling salted water for 15–20 minutes or until tender.

Meanwhile, place the smoked haddock in a large pan, pour over the milk, then cover and bring to the boil. Remove from the heat and leave the fish to finish cooking for another 5 minutes in the hot milk.

Drain the potatoes and return to the pan, then mash well until smooth. Beat in the curry paste, spring onions and herbs.

Transfer the cooked smoked haddock to a plate with a fish slice. Break up the flesh into rough flakes, discarding any skin and bones. Gently fold into the mashed potato mixture. Season to taste.

Using a small ice cream scoop, shape the haddock and potato mixture into 18 even-sized balls, then, using slightly wetted hands, shape into patties. Arrange on a baking sheet and leave to cool completely, then cover with cling film and chill for at least 2 hours (overnight is best) to allow the fish cakes to firm up.

Place the flour on a plate and season generously. Put the beaten eggs into a shallow dish, with the breadcrumbs and sesame seeds in a separate dish. Dust the chilled fish cakes in the seasoned flour, then carefully dip them in the beaten egg, then coat in the sesame breadcrumbs.

Heat the oil in a heavy-based large frying pan and shallow fry the fish cakes in batches for about 4–5 minutes on each side, until crisp and golden. Drain well on kitchen paper and keep warm.

Quickly mix the mayonnaise with the lemon juice and chives in a bowl. Season to taste.

To serve, arrange the fish cakes on warmed plates with the salad and add a dollop of the lemon mayonnaise to each one. Garnish with the lime wedges.

Cheese, tomato and basil macaroni

This is the kind of pasta dish I tend to make when there's nothing much left in the fridge. It really takes no time to prepare and is great served with a light rocket salad and a decent glass of wine.

Serves 4

300 g (11 oz) cherry tomatoes on the vine
1 garlic clove, finely chopped
1 tablespoon olive oil
350 g (12 oz) macaroni pasta
250 g (9 oz) tub mascarpone cheese
2 teaspoons Dijon mustard
2 tablespoons shredded fresh basil
200 g (7 oz) freshly grated Parmesan
salt and freshly ground black pepper

Preheat the oven to 220°C/425°F/gas 7. Carefully remove the cherry tomatoes from the vine and place in an ovenproof dish. Sprinkle with half the garlic and drizzle over the olive oil. Season to taste. Roast for 5 minutes, until the tomatoes have softened slightly and the skins have started to split, tossing once or twice to ensure even cooking.

Meanwhile, cook the macaroni in a large pan of boiling salted water and cook for 8–10 minutes or according to packet instructions, until al dente (tender but firm to the bite).

Place the mascarpone in a bowl and beat in the mustard, basil, Parmesan and the remaining garlic.

Drain the pasta and return to the pan. Stir in the mascarpone cheese mixture, then carefully fold in the roasted cherry tomatoes. Season to taste. Tip into the ovenproof dish that you used for the tomatoes. Bake for 20 minutes until bubbling and golden brown.

To serve, leave the cheese, tomato and basil macaroni to stand for a few minutes, then serve straight from the dish onto warmed plates.

Satay vegetable noodles

Stir-frying is a traditional Chinese cooking technique that is very easy to master. To check if the vegetables are cooked, pierce them with the tip of a knife – the vegetables should feel as soft as butter.

Serves 4–6

RTÉ **GUIDE**

READER TESTED

275 g (10 oz) fine egg noodles
1 tablespoon sunflower oil
1 large red pepper, cored, seeded and thinly sliced
225 g (8 oz) fine green beans, trimmed and halved
175 g (6 oz) baby corn, halved lengthways
2 garlic cloves, crushed
400 g (14 oz) can coconut milk
100 g (4 oz) crunchy peanut butter
2 tablespoons dark soy sauce
2 tablespoons sweet chilli sauce
1 teaspoon light muscovado sugar
juice of ½ lime, pips removed
chopped fresh coriander and finely chopped spring onions, to garnish

Place the fine egg noodles in a pan of boiling water and cook for 3–4 minutes, until tender, or according to packet instructions.

Heat a wok until very hot. Add the oil and swirl around the edges, then tip in the red pepper, green beans, baby corn and garlic and stir-fry for 3–4 minutes, until the vegetables are tender, sprinkling over a tablespoon of water if the mixture is getting too dry.

Drain the noodles and add to the wok with the coconut milk, peanut butter, soy sauce, chilli sauce, sugar and squeeze in the lime juice. Stir fry for another 2–3 minutes, until all of the ingredients are piping hot.

To serve, divide among warmed bowls and scatter over some coriander and spring onions.

Vietnamese beef noodles

This is what I love to eat when I'm feeling a bit under the weather but need my body to keep going. It's a fantastic way of making those thin steaks go a bit further and literally takes no more than 15 minutes to prepare from start to finish.

Serves 4

450 g (1 lb) thin egg noodles
1.2 litres (2 pints) chicken stock
1 teaspoon freshly grated root ginger
sunflower oil
350 g (12 oz) minute steaks (very thinly sliced)
1 tablespoon sweet chilli sauce
150 g (5 oz) baby corn, halved
150 g (5 oz) mangetout, trimmed
200 g (7 oz) pak choi, cut on the diagonal into 4 cm (1 ½ inch) pieces
1 teaspoon cornflour
4 tablespoons dark soy sauce
juice of 1 lime
fresh mint leaves
150 g (5 oz) fresh bean sprouts, well picked over
2 tablespoons chopped fresh salad cress, to garnish

Place the noodles in a heatproof bowl and pour over enough boiling water to cover. Set side for 5 minutes until softened or as per packet instructions.

Pour the stock into a large pan with the ginger and bring to the boil.

Heat a griddle pan until very hot, then lightly oil it. Brush the steaks with the chilli sauce. Place on the hot griddle and cook for 2 minutes on each side. Transfer to a plate and set aside.

Add the baby corn to the stock with the mangetout and pak choi. Mix the cornflour with a little water in a bowl, then stir into the pan. Return to a simmer and cook for 2 minutes, until tender. Add the soy sauce, lime juice and mint, stirring to combine.

To serve, drain the noodles and divide among warmed bowls. Add the bean sprouts and ladle over the flavoured stock. Thinly slice the rested steaks and add to the bowls. Scatter salad cress on top.

Curried chicken in coconut milk

Thai curries are very quick and easy to prepare, especially now that most supermarkets sell authentic ready-made curry pastes flavoured with chilli, ginger, garlic, lemon grass and spices.

Serves 4–6

1 tablespoon sunflower oil
4 skinless chicken breast fillets, sliced
1 large onion, finely chopped
2 garlic cloves, finely chopped
1 teaspoon freshly grated root ginger
2 teaspoons Thai red curry paste
300 ml (½ pint) chicken stock
400 g (14 oz) can coconut milk
2 teaspoons caster sugar
good pinch of salt
juice of 1 lime
chopped fresh coriander leaves, to garnish
Thai fragrant or basmati rice, to serve

Heat a wok until very hot. Add the oil and heat until it is almost smoking, swirling around the sides. Tip in the chicken breast and cook for a few minutes, until lightly browned.

Add the onion, garlic and ginger to the wok and cook for another 3–4 minutes, until softened. Stir in the curry paste and cook for 2 minutes, stirring continuously. Pour in the chicken stock and coconut milk and bring to a gentle simmer. Stir in the sugar and salt.

Add enough lime juice to taste and simmer gently for 10–15 minutes, until the sauce has slightly reduced and the chicken is completely tender.

To serve, divide among warmed wide-rimmed bowls and sprinkle over the coriander, then serve with the Thai fragrant or basmati rice.

Spaghetti Bolognese

This is my foolproof mince recipe, which I use to make lasagne, moussaka and cottage pie. When I go to the trouble of preparing it, I'll always make a really large pot so that I can freeze it in small batches to use when the need arises. If time allows, leave to cool, then chill until the fat solidifies on the top. Carefully remove it and discard.

Serves 4–6

2 tablespoons olive oil
25 g (1 oz) rindless streaky bacon, diced
1 small onion, finely diced
1 celery stick, finely diced
1 carrot, finely diced
2 garlic cloves, crushed
½ teaspoon fresh thyme leaves
1 bay leaf
½ teaspoon dried oregano
450 g (1 lb) lean minced beef (coarsely ground, if possible)
1 tablespoon tomato purée
150 ml (¼ pint) red wine
400 g (14 oz) can chopped tomatoes
600 ml (1 pint) fresh chicken or beef stock
1 teaspoon anchovy essence or 2 canned anchovy fillets, finely minced to a paste (optional)
350 g (12 oz) spaghetti
salt and freshly ground black pepper
freshly grated Parmesan, to serve

Heat a large, heavy-based pan. Add the olive oil and tip in the bacon. Cook for a couple of minutes, until it is crispy and has released some natural fats, then add the onion, celery, carrot, garlic, thyme, bay leaf and oregano and cook over a medium heat until the vegetables have softened and taken on a little colour, stirring occasionally.

Add the minced beef to the pan. Mix until well combined, then sauté until well browned, breaking up any lumps with a wooden spoon. Stir in the tomato purée and continue to cook, stirring for a minute or two.

LIMERICK
COUNTY LIBRARY

Deglaze the pan with a little red wine, scraping up any sediment. Pour in the remaining wine with the tomatoes and stock, then add the anchovy essence or anchovies, if using, and season to taste. Bring to the boil, then reduce the heat and simmer, stirring from time to time, for about 2 hours or up to 4 hours, until the beef is completely tender. Season to taste. If the liquid reduces too much, top up with a little water.

When ready to serve, bring a large pan of water to a rolling boil. Add a good pinch of salt and swirl in the spaghetti. Stir once, then cook for 8–10 minutes, or according to the instructions on the packet, until the pasta is al dente (tender but still firm to the bite). Drain and return to the pan with the Bolognese sauce. Toss until well combined.

To serve, divide the spaghetti Bolognese among warmed wide-rimmed bowls and sprinkle over the Parmesan.

Chunky chicken and potato pie

This recipe would be perfect for leftover turkey at Christmas – just omit chicken and cook as described below, folding in the turkey pieces before leaving the sauce to cool down. If you like a bit of kick to your food, try adding 1 teaspoon of cayenne pepper to the flour.

Serves 4–6

1 tablespoon olive oil
4 large skinless chicken thighs, boned and trimmed
2 potatoes, cut into cubes
2 red onions, cut into wedges
2 leeks, trimmed and thickly sliced
2 garlic cloves, halved
1 bay leaf
1 teaspoon chopped fresh thyme
1 tablespoon plain flour

50 g (2 oz) frozen peas
75 g (3 oz) button mushrooms, cut in half
300 ml (½ pint) crème fraîche
300 ml (½ pint) chicken stock
2 tablespoons chopped fresh flat-leaf parsley
375 g (13 oz) packet ready-rolled puff pastry, thawed if frozen
1 egg, beaten, to glaze
salt and freshly ground black pepper
fresh green salad, to serve

Preheat the oven to 190°C/375°F/gas 5. Put the olive oil in a large pie dish. Add the chicken thighs, potatoes, onions, leeks, garlic, bay leaf, thyme and flour. Toss together well and season to taste. Roast for 25 minutes, until tender, turning the chicken and vegetables occasionally to ensure they cook evenly.

Remove from the oven and fold in the frozen peas and mushrooms, then stir in the crème fraîche, chicken stock and parsley. Leave to cool slightly.

Lay the pastry over the pie dish, tucking the edges down the sides. Brush the rim with water to help it stick, then brush the top of the pie with beaten egg to glaze. Bake in the oven for 25–30 minutes, until the pastry has risen and is golden and the chicken and vegetables are tender. Reduce the temperature of the oven if it's browning too quickly.

To serve, bring the pie directly to the table and serve onto warm plates, handing around a bowl of the fresh green salad so that everyone can help themselves.

Neapolitan pizza

The classic, original pizza – nothing else comes close in terms of simplicity and balance. They are incredibly easy to make using sachets of easy-blend yeast and only need to be left to rise and prove once. These pizzas are a fantastic vehicle for all sorts of toppings, but don't be tempted to overload them or the base will become soggy.

Serves 4

RTE **GUIDE**

READER TESTED

350 g (12 oz) strong white flour, plus extra for dusting
7 g (¼ oz) sachet easy-blend yeast
1 teaspoon salt
2 tablespoons extra virgin olive oil, plus extra for greasing and drizzling
225 ml (8 fl oz) warm water
2 teaspoons semolina or dried white breadcrumbs
8 tablespoons passata rustica (crushed tomatoes)
a few fresh basil leaves, torn
25 g (1 oz) freshly grated Parmesan
150 g (5 oz) ball mozzarella, drained and roughly chopped
salt and freshly ground black pepper
mixed green salad, to serve (optional)

Place the flour, yeast and teaspoon of salt in a food processor fitted with a dough attachment (or use a bowl and a wooden spoon if you don't have a processor). Mix the oil and warm water in a jug. With the motor running, slowly pour in the oil mixture through the feeder tube or stir by hand and mix until you have achieved a soft, stretchy dough. Knead for 5 minutes in the machine or for 10 minutes by hand on a lightly floured work surface.

Transfer the dough to a lightly oiled bowl, rub the top with a little more oil and cover with a clean, damp tea towel. Set aside at room temperature for 1 hour or until the dough has doubled in size.

Preheat the oven to 240°C/475°F/gas 9. Punch the dough down with your fist. Remove the dough from the bowl and knead for a couple of minutes until smooth, then cut in half and roll out each half on a lightly floured surface to a 25 cm (10 inch) circle. Sprinkle the semolina or breadcrumbs onto two large, flat baking sheets and transfer the pizza bases on top.

Season the passata to taste, then spread over the pizza bases, leaving a 1 cm (½ inch) border around the edges. Scatter over the basil, then drizzle over a little olive oil and scatter the Parmesan on top with the mozzarella. Bake for 10–12 minutes, until the bases are crisp and the cheeses are bubbling and lightly golden. Remove from the oven and drizzle over a little more olive oil.

To serve, cut the pizzas into wedges and arrange on warmed plates with some salad.

Variations

Caramelised onion and goat's cheese

Cook three thinly sliced large onions in a little oil for about 30 minutes to 1 hour until caramelised, stirring regularly. Spread over pizza bases and then sprinkle over ¼ teaspoon of chopped fresh rosemary and dot with 100–175 g (4–6 oz) of goat's cheese. Bake and finish as described above.

American hot

Prepare the bases with the passata, basil and olive oil and then scatter over 50 g (2 oz) of thinly sliced pepperoni and 50 g (2 oz) of drained sliced jalapeño chillies (from a jar or can). Bake and finish as described above.

Baking
in the afternoon

White chocolate cupcakes

These cupcakes originated in the US and are very easy to make. You'll find them a massive hit with children and adults alike. If your tin isn't non-stick, simply line with deep paper cases.

Makes 24 cupcakes

250 g (9 oz) butter, at room temperature, plus extra for greasing
250 g (9 oz) caster sugar
175 g (6 oz) self-raising flour, sifted
4 eggs, lightly beaten
1 teaspoon vanilla extract
50 g (2 oz) plain flour, sifted
175 ml (6 fl oz) milk
12 raspberries (optional)

For the white chocolate icing
400 g (14 oz) icing sugar, sifted
100 g (4 oz) white chocolate, broken into pieces
few drops vanilla extract
finely grated rind of 1 orange

Preheat the oven to 180°C/350°F/gas 4. Line 2 bun tins with 24 paper cases. Place the butter and sugar in a bowl and beat until pale and creamy. Add a little of the self-raising flour, then slowly add the eggs and vanilla extract, mixing well to combine.

Slowly add the remaining self-raising and plain flour to the butter and sugar mixture with the milk and beat until just smooth. Divide the mixture between the muffin holes and bake for 25 minutes, until well risen and golden brown. Remove from the oven and leave to sit for 10 minutes in the tin. Turn the cupcakes out onto a wire rack to cool completely.

Meanwhile, make the icing. Mix the icing sugar in a bowl with 1 tablespoon of water to make a thick paste. Melt the white chocolate in the microwave in a heatproof bowl or set over a pan of simmering water. Leave to cool a little, then stir in the icing sugar paste and add the vanilla extract and orange rind, beating with a wooden spoon until smooth.

Cover the cooled cupcakes with the white chocolate icing and top each one with a fresh raspberry.

To serve, arrange on a plate in a pyramid, or wrap in greaseproof paper to take on picnics or in packed lunches.

Butterfly cupcakes

This makes special little cakes, ideal for parties or visiting children. For a chocolate version, replace 25 g (1 oz) of the flour with cocoa powder, then fill with apricot jam and a butter cream made with butter, icing sugar and orange or lemon juice.

Makes 12

125 g (4 ½ oz) unsalted butter, at room temperature
175 g (6 oz) caster sugar
175 g (6 oz) self-raising flour
120 ml (4 fl oz) milk
2 eggs
120 ml (4 fl oz) cream
2 tablespoons strawberry jam
icing sugar, to dust

Preheat the oven to 180°C/350°F/gas 4. Line a bun tin with 12 paper cases. Place the butter and sugar in a bowl with the flour, milk and eggs. Beat with an electric beater on low speed, then increase the speed and beat for 2–3 minutes, until well blended and smooth.

Half-fill the papers cases and bake for 15 minutes or until cooked through and lightly golden. Transfer to a wire rack to cool completely.

Cut shallow rounds from the centre of each cupcake using the point of a sharp knife, then cut in half. Whip the cream in a bowl until soft peaks have formed, then spoon approximately 2 teaspoons of cream into each cavity. Top each one with half a teaspoon of jam and position two halves of the cake tops in the jam to resemble butterfly wings. Dust with icing sugar to finish.

To serve, arrange on plates or wrap loosely in greaseproof paper to take to the park or in packed lunches.

Peanut toffee shortbread

Cut into small squares or bars, this shortbread is always popular. For me, it's the different textures that are the principal appeal – the crunch of the shortbread base with the creamy caramel on top.

Makes about 16 bars

300 g (11 oz) butter, at room temperature, plus extra for greasing
125 g (4 ½ oz) caster sugar
1 egg
175 g (6 oz) plain flour
175 g (6 oz) light muscovado sugar
2 tablespoons golden syrup
½ teaspoon fresh lemon juice
400 g (14 oz) roasted unsalted peanuts

Preheat the oven to 180°C/350°F/gas 4, lightly grease a 18 cm x 27 ½ cm (7 inch x 11 inch) baking tin and line the base and sides with non-stick parchment paper that is hanging over the sides.

Using an electric beater, cream 100 g (4 oz) of the butter with the caster sugar in a bowl until light and fluffy. Add the egg and beat well to combine. Sift the flour into a separate bowl, then fold into the butter mixture using a large metal spoon until just combined. Press into the lined tin and bake for 15 minutes or until firm and very lightly browned. Leave to cool for 10 minutes.

Place the remaining butter in a heavy-based pan with the muscovado sugar, golden syrup and lemon juice. Cook over a low heat for a couple of minutes until the sugar has dissolved, stirring continuously. Increase the heat slightly and simmer for another 5 minutes, stirring.

Remove the toffee from the heat and stir in the peanuts. Using two spoons, spread evenly over the shortbread base, being very careful, as the mixture is extremely hot. Return to the oven for another 5 minutes to help the toffee to set. Remove from the oven and leave to cool in the tin for 15 minutes, then turn out and cut into squares or small bars.

To serve, arrange on plates or wrap in greaseproof paper to take on picnics or in packed lunches.

Sesame and ginger slice

This cake can be cut into whatever size you prefer – large slices for hungry teenagers, or small, two-bite-sized pieces for younger children. I've said it makes 21 slices, but this is just a rough guide. Two can be easily baked at the same time, which means making about 40 portions in one go – much more than you would get from two Victoria sandwiches.

Makes about 21 slices

125 g (4 ½ oz) unsalted butter, at room temperature, plus extra for greasing
125 g (4 ½ oz) plain flour
½ teaspoon bicarbonate of soda
1 teaspoon ground ginger
½ teaspoon ground mixed spice
2 eggs
150 g (5 oz) light muscovado sugar
1 tablespoon chopped crystallised stem ginger (from a jar)
50 g (2 oz) toasted sesame seeds

Preheat the oven to 180°C/350°F/gas 4. Lightly grease a 20 cm x 30 cm (8 inch x 12 inch) shallow baking tin and line the base and sides with non-stick parchment paper that is hanging over the sides. Melt the butter in a small pan or in the microwave. Remove from the heat and leave to cool a little.

Sift the flour in a large bowl with the bicarbonate of soda, ground ginger and mixed spice. Beat the eggs and sugar in a separate large bowl for 2 minutes or until thickened and creamy. Fold into the flour mixture, then add the cooled melted butter with the crystallised ginger and half the sesame seeds, mixing gently to combine.

Spread the mixture into the tin and sprinkle over the remaining sesame seeds in an even layer. Bake for 20 minutes or until firm to the touch and slightly coloured. Leave to cool in the tin for 10 minutes, then cut into slices and lift out with a palette knife. Leave to cool completely on a wire rack.

To serve, arrange on a plate or wrap in greaseproof paper to take on picnics or in packed lunches.

Madeleines

For these shell-shaped cakes (from my good friend Lea Linster), you'll need a Madeleine tin 7 ½ cm (3 inches) long x 3 cm (1 ¼ inches) wide, available from specialist kitchen shops or by mail order. They don't keep particularly well, so are best on the day that they are made, but the raw mixture will keep well in the fridge for a couple of weeks so that you can make them as you need them.

Makes 24

225 g (8 oz) butter, plus extra melted butter for greasing
75 g (3 oz) plain flour, plus extra for dusting
225 g (8 oz) egg whites, at room temperature (about 4 in total)
225 g (8 oz) icing sugar
100 g (4 oz) ground almonds

Lightly grease a 12-hole Madeleine tin with melted butter, then dust with flour, shaking off any excess. Place in the fridge for at least 2 hours, but overnight is best.

Preheat the oven to 200°C/400°F/gas 6. Place the butter in a small pan and allow to brown slightly. Remove from the heat and leave to cool.

Sift the flour into a large bowl. Add the egg whites, icing sugar and ground almonds. Using an electric mixer, beat until well combined and smooth. Slowly add the melted brown butter and mix for 5 minutes, until smooth and thickened.

Spoon the mixture into the prepared tin so that it is nearly level with the tops, leaving a little room for rising. Bake for 10–12 minutes (small Madeleines will only take 7 minutes), until well risen, golden and springy to the touch. Remove from the oven and leave to rest in the tin for 2 minutes, then ease out of the tins with a palette knife. Leave on a wire rack to cool slightly.

To serve, arrange on plates and enjoy with coffee or a cup of tea.

Passion fruit creams

These cookies are not quite as crisp as a biscuit and they won't keep for long, a couple of days at most. Passion fruit pulp is obtained by scooping out the flesh from a couple of ripe passion fruit. It can then be used as it is, seeds and all, or passed through a sieve for a smoother finish. Otherwise the finely grated rind of an orange or lemon works well.

Makes 14

250 g (9 oz) butter, at room temperature
40 g (1 ½ oz) icing sugar
1 teaspoon vanilla extract
175 g (6 oz) self-raising flour
50 g (2 oz) custard powder

For the passion fruit filling
50 g (2 oz) butter, at room temperature
50 g (2 oz) icing sugar
2 tablespoons passion fruit pulp

Preheat the oven to 160°C/325°F/gas 3. Line 2 baking sheets with non-stick parchment paper. Beat the butter and sugar in a bowl until light and creamy. Add the vanilla extract, then sift in the flour and custard powder. Mix to a soft dough. Roll level tablespoons of the mixture into 28 balls and place on the lined baking sheets, flattening each one slightly with a fork.

Bake the cookies for 20 minutes or until lightly golden. Leave to cool on the baking sheets for 5 minutes, then transfer to a wire rack to cool completely.

Meanwhile, make the passion fruit filling. Beat the butter and sugar in a bowl until light and creamy, then beat in the passion fruit pulp. Spread or pipe half of the cookies with the passion fruit filling, then sandwich the remaining biscuits together. Leave to firm up for at least 1 hour.

To serve, arrange on a plate or wrap in greaseproof paper to take on picnics or in packed lunches.

Pecan and white chocolate brownies

Brownies are likely to dip in the middle, but this adds to their charm.
Don't be tempted to overcook, as it's much better to have a slightly gooey
texture. The outside crust should be on the crisp side, though, because
of the high proportion of sugar.

Makes 12

40 g (1 ½ oz) butter, plus extra for greasing
225 g (8 oz) caster sugar
2 eggs
1 teaspoon vanilla extract
150 g (5 oz) white chocolate buttons
100 g (4 oz) self-raising flour
½ teaspoon baking powder
125 g (4 ½ oz) pecan nuts, roughly chopped

Preheat the oven to 180°C/350°F/gas 4. Grease an 18 cm (7 inch) square tin
and line the base with non-stick parchment paper that is hanging over the edges.
Melt the butter in a small pan or in the microwave. Leave to cool a little.

Using an electric beater, beat the sugar, eggs and vanilla extract in a bowl
until thickened and doubled in volume. Melt half of the white chocolate in the
microwave or in a bowl set over a pan of simmering water. Leave to cool a little,
then stir into the egg mixture.

Sift the flour and baking powder into a separate bowl, then fold into the egg
mixture. Finally, fold in the remaining chocolate buttons and the pecans. Pour
into the prepared tin and smooth the surface. Bake for 30–35 minutes or until
firm to the touch and the mixture comes away from the sides of the tin. Leave
to cool in the tin. When the brownies are completely cold, cut into squares.

To serve, arrange on plates or wrap in greaseproof paper to take on picnics or
in packed lunches.

Chocolate chip cookies

American-style cookies laden with dark chocolate make a delicious accompaniment to tea or coffee. Make them on a rainy afternoon and eat them while still warm from the oven. If there are any left, they can be stored in an airtight tin for up to 1 week.

Makes about 24

125 g (4 ½ oz) butter, at room temperature
150 g (5 oz) light muscovado sugar
1 teaspoon vanilla extract
1 egg, beaten
1 tablespoon milk
225 g (8 oz) plain flour
1 teaspoon baking powder
125 g (4 ½ oz) plain chocolate (drops or bar cut into small chunks no larger than 1 cm/½ inch)
125 g (4 ½ oz) white chocolate (drops or bar cut into small chunks no larger than 1 cm/½ inch)

Preheat the oven to 180°C/350°F/gas 4. Line a large baking sheet with non-stick parchment paper.

Cream the butter and sugar in a large bowl with an electric beater. Add the vanilla extract and egg and beat again until well combined. Stir in the milk.

Sift the flour and baking powder into a bowl, then fold into the butter and egg mixture. Stir in the plain and white chocolate drops or chunks.

Drop level tablespoons of the cookie mixture onto the lined baking sheet, leaving enough room between them so that they can spread out, then gently press with a fork. Bake for 10–12 minutes or until lightly golden. Leave on the baking sheet for 5 minutes, then transfer to a wire rack to cool.

To serve, arrange on plates or wrap in greaseproof paper and pack for picnics or lunchboxes.

Caramel ripple crumbles

These delicious morsels melt in the mouth. They are irresistible to chocoholics and can be served as an afternoon cake or as a pudding with single cream or ice cream. They are also very portable, so are perfect for a picnic or lunchbox.

Makes 12

100 g (4 oz) plain chocolate (good-quality)
100 g (4 oz) butter, plus extra for greasing
2 eggs, beaten
150 g (5 oz) light muscovado sugar
50 g (2 oz) plain flour

For the caramel ripple
200 g (7 oz) soft cream cheese
50 g (2 oz) dark muscovado sugar
few drops vanilla extract
1 egg

Preheat the oven to 160°C/325°F/gas 3. Grease a 20 cm (8 inch) square shallow cake tin and line the base with non-stick parchment paper that is hanging over the edges.

Break up the chocolate into a heatproof bowl and add the butter. Set on top of a pan of gently simmering water and leave to melt, stirring from time to time.

Meanwhile, prepare the caramel ripple mixture. Combine the soft cream cheese, dark muscovado sugar, vanilla extract and egg in a bowl and mix well until evenly blended. Set aside.

Stir the beaten eggs into the chocolate mixture with the light muscovado sugar. Sift the flour into a separate bowl, then fold in. Spoon half of the chocolate mixture into the prepared tin; then dollop alternate teaspoons of the caramel mixture and the remaining chocolate mixture on top. Using a skewer, lightly ripple together to make a marbled top.

Bake for 25–30 minutes, until just set. Leave to cool in the tin for 5–10 minutes before cutting into squares, then transfer to a wire rack with a palette knife to cool completely.

To serve, arrange on plates or wrap in greaseproof paper to take on picnics or in packed lunches.

Bakewell slice

Be generous with the raspberries, it makes all the difference to this teatime treat. There's no need to line or grease the baking sheet, as the pastry already has enough fat and there's no sugar in it to make it stick.

Serves 8

300 g (11 oz) ready-made shortcrust pastry, thawed if frozen
a little plain flour, for dusting
50 g (2 oz) butter, at room temperature
50 g (2 oz) golden caster sugar
1 egg, beaten
125 g (4 ½ oz) ground almonds
few drops vanilla extract
250 g (9 oz) raspberries
50 g (2 oz) flaked almonds
1 tablespoon icing sugar
whipped cream, to serve

Preheat the oven to 200°C/400°F/gas 6. Roll out the pastry into two 27 ½ cm x 7 ½ cm (11 inch x 3 inch) rectangles on a lightly floured board. Place on non-stick baking sheets and prick all over with a fork. Bake for 5 minutes, until set but not coloured.

Meanwhile, using an electric mixer, beat the butter and sugar together in a bowl until pale and fluffy. Stir in the egg, ground almonds and vanilla extract to make a stiff paste.

Spread the almond paste on top of the pastry, leaving a border around the edges. Gently press the raspberries onto the paste, scatter over the flaked almonds and sift the icing sugar on top. Bake for 20–25 minutes, until puffed up and lightly golden.

Leave on the baking sheets for a few minutes, then carefully transfer to a wire rack to cool.

To serve, cut into slices and arrange on plates with dollops of whipped cream.

Coconut squares

Made with ground rice, hazelnuts and coconut, these tasty cakes are gluten free. They are ideal for freezing or will last well wrapped in greaseproof paper and stored in an airtight container for up to 5 days.

Makes 12

75 g (3 oz) butter, at room temperature, plus extra for greasing
200 g (7 oz) Demerara sugar
175 g (6 oz) ground rice
2 eggs
pinch salt
few drops vanilla extract
75 g (3 oz) desiccated coconut
75 g (3 oz) skinned hazelnuts, chopped
4 tablespoons raspberry jam
3 tablespoons apricot jam

Preheat the oven to 180°C/350°F/gas 4. Grease a 27 ½ cm x 18 cm (11 inch x 7 inch) shallow baking tin. Cream the butter and 75 g (3 oz) of the sugar together in a bowl until light and fluffy. Stir in 150 g (5 oz) of the ground rice. Spread the mixture into the prepared tin and bake for 15 minutes, until firm to the touch but not coloured. Leave to cool for a few minutes.

Meanwhile, lightly beat the eggs in a bowl. Add the remaining sugar and ground rice with the salt, vanilla extract, desiccated coconut and chopped hazelnuts, mixing well to combine.

Spread the raspberry jam over the slightly cooled base, then cover with an even layer of the coconut mixture. Bake for another 20 minutes, until lightly golden and firm to the touch. Allow to cool slightly.

Warm the apricot jam in the microwave or in a small pan, then brush all over the top of the cake. Cut into even-sized squares. Leave to cool completely in the tin, then transfer with a palette knife on to greaseproof paper. Wrap up and store in an airtight container.

To serve, arrange on a plate, or bring on a picnic or put into lunchboxes wrapped individually in greaseproof paper.

Vanilla and apricot patties

These quick and easy patty cakes are irresistibly moist. They are great as part of an afternoon tea or can be served warm with crème fraîche or thick cream as a dessert. If your muffin tin isn't non-stick, then line with deep paper cases.

Makes 12

175 g (6 oz) butter, plus extra for greasing
75 g (3 oz) self-raising flour
175 g (6 oz) ground almonds
175 g (6 oz) golden caster sugar
1 teaspoon of vanilla essence
4 egg whites
12 ready-to-eat dried apricots
icing sugar, to dust
crème fraîche or whipped cream, to serve

Preheat the oven to 200°C/400°F/gas 6. Lightly grease a non-stick 12-hole muffin or deep bun tin. Melt the butter in the microwave or in a small pan and leave to cool slightly.

Sift the flour into a bowl and mix in the ground almonds and sugar. Make a well in the centre and add the vanilla essence, egg whites and melted butter, stirring well, until evenly combined.

Divide the cake mixture evenly among the tin sections. Gently place an apricot on each cake and bake for 15–20 minutes, until well risen and golden brown. Leave for about 10 minutes to firm up slightly, then run a knife around the edges of the patties to loosen them from the tin. Transfer to a wire rack to cool completely.

To serve, arrange warm or cold on plates with a light dusting of icing sugar. Hand around a bowl of crème fraîche or whipped cream to allow your guests to help themselves.

Mango and maple cake

This is a moist loaf cake which needs no buttering. Store it in the fridge if you want to keep it for any length of time. If you can't get hold of decent ripe mangoes, use two drained cans of mango in natural juice.

Serves 8

125 g (4 ½ oz) butter
150 g (5 oz) light muscovado sugar
100 g (4 oz) maple syrup
150 g (5 oz) plain flour
100 g (4 oz) wholemeal flour
2 teaspoons baking powder
1 teaspoon ground cinnamon
2 ripe mangoes, peeled, stoned and finely chopped
100 g (4 oz) pecan nuts, roughly chopped

For the topping
finely grated rind and juice of 1 orange
200 g (7 oz) soft cream cheese
50 g (2 oz) icing sugar
½ vanilla pod, split in half and seeds scraped out

Preheat the oven to 160°C/325°F/gas 3. Place the butter, sugar and maple syrup in a small pan and heat gently until melted, stirring occasionally.

Sift the plain and wholemeal flour together into a large bowl with the baking powder and cinnamon, then tip in any remaining bran that is left in the sieve. Stir in the melted syrup mixture, then fold in the mangoes and pecan nuts.

Spoon the mixture into a non-stick 900 g (2 lb) loaf tin and bake for 1 ½ hours, until well risen and golden brown. To test if the cake is done, stick a fine metal skewer into the centre of the cake – it should come out clean. Leave the cake to cool in the tin for 5 minutes, then turn out onto a wire rack and leave to cool completely.

To make the topping, mix the orange rind in a bowl with the soft cream cheese, icing sugar and vanilla seeds, then stir in enough of the orange juice to make a smooth icing. Spread thickly over the top of the cooked cake.

To serve, cut the mango and maple cake into slices and serve on plates.

Rhubarb and ginger crumble cake

This versatile cake is best served warm as a pudding or cold as a teatime treat. I like it with whipped cream, but it would also be good with crème fraîche, clotted cream, vanilla ice cream or custard. If you don't fancy the rhubarb, try using apples or blackberries, depending on the time of year.

Serves 6–8

For the crumble
125 g (4 ½ oz) plain flour
4 tablespoons caster sugar
75 g (3 oz) butter, at room temperature
pinch ground cinnamon

For the fruit
750 g (1 ¾ lb) rhubarb, cut into 1 cm (½ inch) pieces
1 tablespoon caster sugar
1 teaspoon ground ginger

For the cake
175 g (6 oz) butter, at room temperature, plus extra for greasing
175 g (6 oz) caster sugar
3 eggs, beaten
175 g (6 oz) plain flour
2 teaspoons baking powder
1 tablespoon milk
whipped cream, to serve

Heat the oven to 190°C/375°F/gas 5. Butter a 23 cm (9 inch) springform cake tin and line the base with non-stick parchment paper.

To make the rhubarb crumble topping, place the flour, sugar, butter and cinnamon in a food processor and pulse until crumbly. To prepare the fruit, place the rhubarb in a bowl and tip in the sugar and ginger. Toss until evenly coated. Set both aside.

To make the cake, beat the butter and sugar together in a bowl until light and fluffy. Beat in the eggs a little at a time, adding 1 tablespoon of the flour when you have added about half of the beaten eggs – this will stop curdling. Sift over the rest of the flour and the baking powder and fold gently but thoroughly. Finally, fold in the milk.

Spread the cake mixture over the base of the prepared cake tin, pile the sugared rhubarb on top, then sprinkle over the crumble topping. Bake for about 1 hour, until the sides of the cake have shrunk slightly away from the tin, the rhubarb is soft and the crumble is golden brown. To test if the cake is done, insert a fine metal skewer into the middle – if it comes out clean, the cake is ready. Remove from the oven and leave to cool in the tin for 15 minutes set on a wire rack.

To serve, cut the rhubarb and ginger crumble cake into slices and arrange on plates with a dollop of whipped cream.

Chocolate and hazelnut raspberry meringue

This cake is a real favourite of mine, the raspberries, hazelnuts and chocolate being a particularly good combination. Fill the meringue about 3 hours before serving; it will then cut into portions without splintering. I've decorated it with white chocolate shavings, which can be very easily made using a thick bar of white chocolate and a potato peeler.

Serves 6–8

100 g (4 oz) skinned toasted hazelnuts
6 egg whites
pinch salt
350 g (12 oz) caster sugar
3 teaspoons sifted cocoa powder

For the filling
300 ml (½ pint) cream
250 g (9 oz) raspberries

For the chocolate sauce
50 g (2 oz) plain chocolate, broken into pieces
2 tablespoons cream
white chocolate shavings, to decorate
icing sugar, to dust

Preheat the oven to 180°C/350°F/gas 4. Line 2 baking sheets with non-stick parchment paper. Draw a 20 cm (8 inch) circle on each piece of paper. Place the toasted hazelnuts in a food processor and pulse until roughly chopped. Set aside.

Place the egg whites in a large bowl with the salt. Whisk on maximum speed with an electric whisk until stiff. Add the sugar a tablespoon at a time and continue whisking, still at top speed, until the mixture is very stiff, stands in peaks and all the sugar has been added. It should be stiff enough for you to hold the bowl over your head upside down! Fold in the reserved chopped hazelnuts with the sieved cocoa powder.

Divide the meringue mixture between the two circles, spreading into rounds of an even thickness using a spatula. Bake for 5 minutes, then reduce the oven temperature to 110°C/225°F/gas ¼ and bake for 1 hour, until the tops of the meringue are crisp and the insides are soft, like a marshmallow. Switch off the oven, then open the oven door slightly and leave the meringues to dry out for another 30 minutes. Slide the meringues, which are still on the parchment, off the baking sheet onto wire racks and leave to cool completely, then peel off the parchment paper.

Whip the cream in a bowl until it holds its shape and use to sandwich the meringues together along with the raspberries. Melt the chocolate and cream in a small pan over a gentle heat, stirring constantly until smooth. Leave to cool.

To serve, decorate the top of the meringue with the white chocolate shavings, then dust with the icing sugar. Bring straight to the table, then cut into slices and arrange on plates with a swirl of the chocolate sauce.

Special Occasion menus

St Patrick's Day
lunch

Smoked salmon and crab tart

You can make the pastry case for the tart up to 24 hours in advance, but if you're short of time, use shop-bought pastry or a ready-made pastry case instead. I often make double the quantity of pastry and make two pastry cases. Shove one in the freezer, then you can just defrost as needed. If you have any pastry left over, use it to make baby quiches or cheese straws.

Serves 6

For the pastry
225 g (8 oz) plain flour, plus extra for dusting
100 g (4 oz) butter, diced and chilled
pinch dried chilli flakes
3 tablespoons ice cold water
salt and freshly ground black pepper
crisp garden salad, to serve

For the tart
a little egg wash, for brushing
150 ml (¼ pint) cream
150 ml (¼ pint) milk
2 tablespoons sweet chilli sauce
2 eggs
2 egg yolks
1 tablespoon snipped fresh chives
200 g (7 oz) smoked salmon, cut into strips
200 g (7 oz) white crab meat
100 g (4 oz) freshly grated Parmesan

RTÉ **GUIDE**
READER TESTED

Preheat the oven to 200°C/400°F/gas 6. To make the pastry, place the flour, butter and chilli flakes in a food processor. Add half a teaspoon of salt and whizz briefly until the mixture forms fine crumbs. Pour in the water through the feeder tube and pulse again so that the pastry comes together. Knead lightly on a lightly floured surface for a few seconds to produce a smooth dough. Wrap in cling film and chill for at least 10 minutes before rolling (or up to 1 hour if time allows).

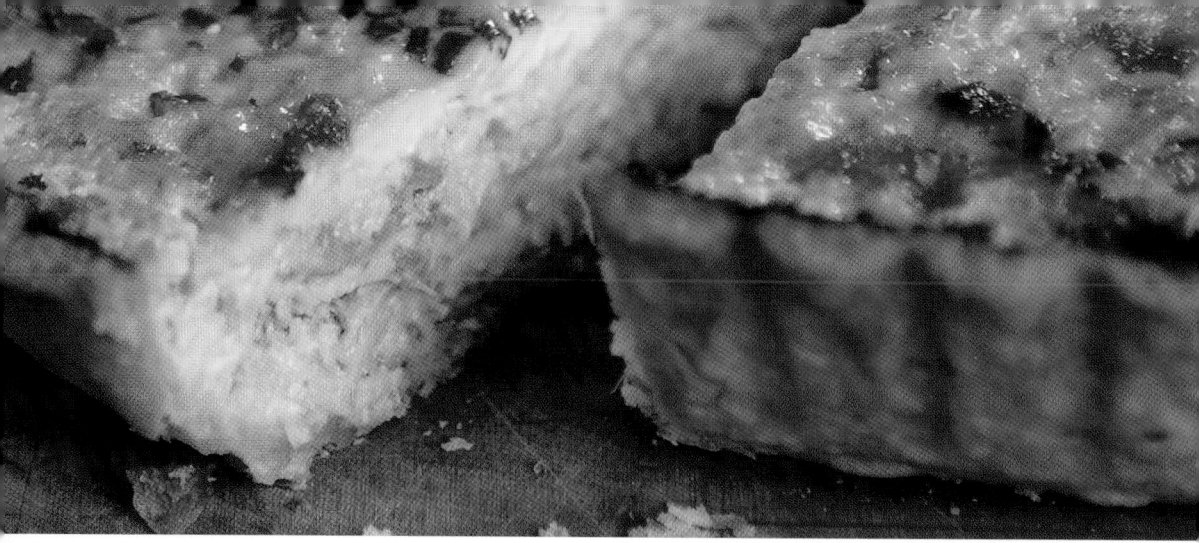

Roll out the pastry on a lightly floured surface and use to line a loose-bottomed 21 cm (8 ½ inch) fluted flan tin that is about 4 cm (1 ½ inches) deep. Use a rolling pin to lift the pastry into the tin, pressing well into the sides and letting the pastry overhang a little, as this prevents shrinkage. Chill for another 10 minutes for the pastry to rest.

Prick the pastry base with a fork, then line with a circle of oiled foil or non-stick parchment paper that is first crumpled up to make it easier to handle. Fill with baking beans or dried pulses and bake for 10 minutes, until the pastry case looks set but not coloured. Carefully remove the foil or paper and lower the temperature to 160°C/325°F/gas 3, then brush with the egg wash to form a seal. Return to the oven for another 5 minutes, or until the base is firm to the touch and the sides are lightly coloured.

Beat together the cream in a bowl with the milk, chilli sauce, eggs and egg yolks until well combined. Stir in the chives and season to taste. Scatter the smoked salmon and crab meat in the bottom of the pastry case and sprinkle the Parmesan on top, then pour in the cream mixture and bake for about 25 minutes, until the filling is just set but still slightly wobbly in the middle. Leave to rest for 5 minutes in the tin, then remove and trim down the excess pastry.

To serve, carefully cut the smoked salmon and crab tart into slices. Arrange on plates with the crisp garden salad.

Irish stew

I never tire of a bowl of steaming hot stew. It's the attention to detail that makes this dish one of the world's great classics. This is my version that I have developed over the years. Of course, it's a meal in itself, but for a special celebration, try serving it buffet style with steaming hot bowls of turnip mash, colcannon and glazed parsnips and carrots and watch your guests' faces light up!

Serves 6

900 g (2 lb) boneless lamb neck, trimmed and cut into cubes
50 g (2 oz) pearl barley, washed
225 g (8 oz) potatoes, cut into chunks
225 g (8 oz) carrots, thickly sliced
225 g (8 oz) leeks, well trimmed and thickly sliced
225 g (8 oz) baby pearl onions, peeled
100 g (4 oz) rindless piece of smoked bacon, diced
2 fresh thyme sprigs

For the lamb stock
450 g (1 lb) lamb bones
1 carrot, cut into cubes
1 onion, sliced
2 whole peppercorns
1 bouquet garni (bundle of herbs tied together with string)
salt and freshly ground black pepper
chopped fresh parsley, to garnish
turnip mash with crispy bacon and onion (page 110), colcannon (page 111) and glazed parsnips and carrots (page 108), to serve

To make the stock, place the lamb bones in a large pan with the carrot, onion, peppercorns and bouquet garni. Cover with cold water and bring to the boil, then reduce the heat and simmer gently for 2 hours, until you have achieved a good flavour. Leave to cool, then skim off any scum and/or fat and strain into a large jug. Cover with cling film and chill until needed.

Place the boneless lamb pieces in a large, clean, heavy-based pan and pour over the reserved stock. Bring to the boil, then skim off any scum from the surface and then stir in the barley. Reduce the heat and simmer for 50 minutes, until slightly reduced and the lamb is almost tender.

Add the potatoes to the lamb with the carrots, leeks, baby pearl onions, smoked bacon and thyme and simmer for 30 minutes or until the lamb and vegetables are completely tender but still holding their shape. Season to taste.

Transfer the stew into a warmed casserole dish and scatter over the parsley. Have dishes of the turnip mash with crispy bacon and onion, colcannon and glazed parsnips and carrots alongside and allow everyone to help themselves.

Glazed parsnips and carrots

The natural sweetness of the carrots and parsnips is picked up by the honey, and the result makes the perfect accompaniment for my Irish stew. This is really very simple to prepare and needs very little looking after.

Serves 6

2 tablespoons olive oil
450 g (1 lb) carrots, trimmed and cut into chunks
450 g (1 lb) parsnips, trimmed, quartered, cored and cut into chunks
1 teaspoon chopped fresh thyme
3 tablespoons clear honey
good dash kecap manis or dark soy sauce
salt and freshly ground black pepper
chopped fresh flat-leaf parsley, to garnish

Preheat the oven to 180°C/350°F/gas 4. Place the oil in a large roasting tin and add the carrots and parsnips. Sprinkle over the thyme and toss everything together until well coated. Season generously. Roast for 30–40 minutes, until tender and just beginning to caramelise.

Drizzle the honey over the carrot and parsnip mixture and add a good dash of the kecap manis or soy sauce, then toss until evenly coated. Roast for another 10 minutes or until the vegetables are just beginning to catch and caramelise around the edges.

To serve, spoon into a warmed dish and scatter over the parsley.

Turnip mash with crispy bacon and onion

Turnips (also known as swedes) are one of my favourite winter vegetables. At the beginning of the season, the small specimens only need the thinnest layer of skin removed, but once they increase in size, you really need to peel away quite a thick layer to get rid of the hard, woody skin.

Serves 6

900 g (2 lb) turnip, peeled and cut into 2 ½ cm (1 inch) chunks
1 tablespoon sunflower oil
1 small onion, finely chopped
50 g (2 oz) rindless piece of smoked bacon, diced
50 g (2 oz) butter
salt and freshly ground black pepper

Place the turnip chunks in a steamer set above a pan of simmering water and season with salt. Cover and cook for about 10 minutes, until tender.

Meanwhile, heat the sunflower oil in a frying pan and gently sauté the onion and bacon until the bacon is crisp and lightly golden and the onion has just begun to colour around the edges.

When the turnip is cooked, roughly mash with the butter. Season to taste, adding plenty of black pepper.

To serve, pile the turnip mash into a warmed dish. Sprinkle the crispy bacon and onion on top.

Colcannon

This is my standard colcannon recipe, which, once mastered, can be adapted for different results. Try replacing a couple of tablespoons of the milk with crème fraîche or use a carton of quark (skimmed-milk soft cheese). I also like adding a couple of tablespoons of chives or a good dollop of Dijon mustard, depending on what you are serving it with.

Serves 6

500 g (1 lb 2 oz) floury potatoes, scrubbed (as evenly sized as possible)
½ Savoy cabbage, cored and thinly shredded
100 ml (3 ½ fl oz) milk
50 g (2 oz) butter
2 spring onions, finely chopped
salt and freshly ground white pepper

Place the unpeeled potatoes in a pan of salted water and bring to the boil. Reduce the heat and simmer for 20–25 minutes or until tender. Drain and return to the pan, then cover with a tea towel for 5 minutes to dry off. Leave to cool slightly.

Meanwhile, blanch the shredded cabbage in a separate pan of boiling salted water for 2–3 minutes until tender but still crisp. Drain well and refresh under cold running water.

Pour the milk into a small pan and add the butter and spring onions. Warm gently for a few minutes without boiling – you want the spring onions to remain crunchy.

Peel the cooked potatoes and mash well, using a potato ricer into a clean pan. Gradually pour in the warm milk mixture, beating continuously with a wooden spoon to combine. Fold in the blanched cabbage and then gently reheat, stirring constantly. Season to taste.

To serve, place the colcannon into a warmed bowl and enjoy.

Pear, ginger and whiskey cake

Hot or cold, this dessert is a knockout! You can make it several hours in advance and leave it to cool. This gives the juices time to be well absorbed into the pears and allows the toffee to set slightly. Otherwise it will keep for 5–6 days in an airtight container.

Serves 6–8

For the topping
75 g (3 oz) butter
125 g (4 ½ oz) light muscovado sugar
2 tablespoons whiskey
4 ripe fat pears

For the gingerbread
100 g (4 oz) butter
175 g (6 oz) plain flour
½ teaspoon baking soda
1 tablespoon ground cinnamon
2 teaspoons ground ginger
½ teaspoon ground nutmeg
pinch ground cloves
2 eggs, beaten
175 g (6 oz) light muscovado sugar
125 g (4 ½ oz) black treacle
200 ml (7 fl oz) milk
2 tablespoons whiskey
whipped cream, to serve

Preheat the oven to 180°C/350°F/gas 4. Butter a 23 cm (9 inch) non-stick springform cake tin and line the base with non-stick parchment paper.

To make the topping, melt the butter and sugar together in a small pan over a medium-low heat until bubbling, then continue to cook for a few minutes, until creamy and toffee coloured, stirring occasionally. Add the whiskey to the pan, swirling to combine. Pour into the cake tin, tipping the tin to spread the whiskey toffee evenly over the base.

Peel the pears, then cut in half and cut out their stalk and cores. Arrange the pears cut side down on top of the toffee mixture, with the stalk ends pointing in towards the centre.

To make the gingerbread, melt the butter in a small pan or in the microwave, then set aside to cool slightly. Sift the flour into a large bowl with the baking soda, cinnamon, ginger, nutmeg and cloves.

In a separate bowl, mix the reserved melted butter with the beaten eggs, sugar, treacle, milk and whiskey. Make a well in the centre of the flour mixture and gradually add the liquid, mixing gently to make a smooth batter. Pour into the tin over the pears. Bake for about 45–55 minutes or until a toothpick or skewer pushed into the middle of the pudding comes out barely moist.

Transfer to a wire rack and leave the pudding to cool for a few minutes, then run a knife around the edge of the cake to make sure it isn't sticking.

Put on some oven gloves and place a large plate on top of the cake tin. Turn the whole thing over as quickly as possible.

To serve, cut into slices and arrange on plates while still warm. Add a dollop of whipped cream to each one.

MacNean chocolate truffles

These truffles make the perfect end to a special lunch served with an Irish coffee (see page 139). However, they also make wonderful gifts for your friends. Experiment with different flavours and try adding rum, Cointreau or whiskey instead of Bailey's.

Makes about 40

250 ml (9 fl oz) cream
250 g (9 oz) butter
500 g (1 lb 2 oz) plain chocolate, broken into squares
2 tablespoons Bailey's Irish cream

For the coating
225 g (8 oz) plain chocolate, broken into squares (minimum 55% cocoa solids)
cocoa powder, for dusting

Place the cream and butter in a pan and bring to the boil. Reduce the heat, then whisk in the chocolate until smooth and melted. Stir in the Bailey's and transfer to a bowl. Leave to cool completely, then cover with cling film and chill for 2–3 hours, until set firm, stirring occasionally to prevent a skin from forming.

When the mixture is cold and set, scoop into small balls – you can use a large melon baller for this. Make sure to dip the melon baller in hot water to give the chocolate mixture a better shape. Arrange on a baking sheet lined with non-stick parchment paper.

To make the coating, melt the chocolate in a heatproof bowl set over a pan of simmering water or in the microwave. Leave to cool a little, then dip the truffles in the melted chocolate and quickly roll in the cocoa powder. Cover with cling film and place in the fridge to set.

To serve, arrange the truffles on a plate to hand around to guests while they are enjoying their coffee.

Easter
lunch

Bruschetta

Bruschetta makes delicious simple nibbles and can look very impressive laid out on platters. Alternatively, use slices of French batons to make little bruschetta (i.e. crostini). Don't be tempted to make these too far in advance, as the bread goes soggy.

Serves 4–6

6 thick slices country bread, preferably sourdough
1 garlic clove, halved
2 tablespoons extra virgin olive oil

Preheat the grill or a griddle pan and use to toast the bread on both sides. Remove from the heat and immediately rub one side with a piece of garlic. To serve, drizzle over the olive oil and have either on its own, or with one of the following delicious toppings, arranged on large serving platters or trays.

Parma ham with basil dressing

Arrange slices of Parma ham on the bruschetta. Whizz one small garlic clove with 4 tablespoons of toasted pine nuts and a good handful of fresh basil leaves in a mini blender. Pour in enough extra virgin olive oil to make a smooth, thickish dressing and fold in a handful of freshly grated Parmesan or Pecorino. Season to taste and drizzle over the Parma ham to serve.

Guacamole

Halve two avocadoes. Remove the stones and scoop out the flesh into a bowl. Mash until smooth, then season with 1 teaspoon of onion salt and plenty of freshly ground black pepper. Stir in a handful of diced semi-sun-dried tomatoes and a couple of finely chopped spring onions, then spread thickly on the bruschetta to serve.

Cherry tomato and mozzarella

Mix 1 teaspoon of balsamic vinegar into a bowl with 3 tablespoons of extra virgin olive oil and season to taste. Stir in 275 g (10 oz) mozzarella cubes with 175 g (6 oz) halved cherry or baby plum tomatoes with a handful of torn fresh basil leaves. Arrange wild rocket leaves on the bruschetta and spoon over the mozzarella and tomato mixture to serve.

Leg of lamb with salsa verde stuffing

Ask your butcher to bone the leg of lamb for you, but to leave the shank end intact. This not only improves the flavour, but also makes carving much easier. For a more pronounced flavour, stud the lamb all over with slivers of garlic and tiny rosemary sprigs. I often add baby carrots to the joint for the last 15–20 minutes, depending on their size.

Serves 4–6

1 leg of lamb, 2 ¼–2 ¾ kg (5–6 lb), boned with shank end left intact

For the stuffing
175 g (6 oz) fresh white breadcrumbs
50 g (2 oz) bunch fresh flat-leaf parsley, leaves stripped and finely chopped
1 tablespoon rinsed capers
4 anchovy fillets, drained and finely chopped
50 g (2 oz) prosciutto, finely chopped (or dried Italian ham)
1 garlic clove, crushed
1 teaspoon Dijon mustard
1 tablespoon fresh lemon juice
50 ml (2 fl oz) olive oil

For the gravy
1 tablespoon plain flour
1 teaspoon tomato purée
100 ml (3 ½ fl oz) red wine
50 ml (2 fl oz) balsamic vinegar
200 ml (7 fl oz) beef or lamb stock
3 tablespoons redcurrant jelly
2 fresh rosemary sprigs
salt and freshly ground pepper

Potato gratin (page 121), sautéed green beans with olive oil and garlic (page 122) and roasted balsamic beetroot (page 123), to serve

Preheat the oven to 190°C/375°F/gas 5. To make the stuffing, place the breadcrumbs in a bowl and add the parsley, capers, anchovies, prosciutto and garlic.

In a separate bowl, whisk together the Dijon, lemon juice and olive oil. Fold into the breadcrumb mixture to moisten it a little. Season to taste.

Press the stuffing inside the boned-out leg of lamb and season the joint all over, then tie up securely and neatly with string. Place the lamb joint in a roasting tin, cover loosely with foil and roast for 1 ½ hours, then remove the foil and baste well. Roast for another 30 minutes, until just tender. If you like your lamb more well done, give it another 30 minutes' cooking time. To check that it is cooked to your liking, insert a skewer into the thickest part of the meat and watch the juice run out – the pinker the juice, the rarer the meat. When it is cooked to your liking, transfer to a carving platter and leave to rest in a warm place for 30 minutes.

To make the gravy, place the roasting tin directly on the hob and stir in the flour. Cook for 1 minute, stirring continuously, then gradually stir in the tomato purée, wine, vinegar and stock, whisking until smooth after each addition and scraping the bottom of the tin to remove any sediment. Transfer to a small pan and whisk in the redcurrant jelly and add the rosemary, then simmer gently until you have achieved the desired consistency.

To serve, when the lamb is rested, carefully cut away the string, then carve into slices, holding the shank end of the bone. Arrange the lamb on warmed plates and spoon over a little of the gravy. Pour the remainder into a gravy jug. Serve with the potato gratin, sautéed green beans and roasted balsamic beetroot.

Potato gratin

The wonderful thing about this delicious potato gratin is that it can be made in advance and reheated in individual portions on a baking sheet for about 20 minutes at the same oven temperature as the lamb is cooked in. Each portion should have a crisp, golden brown crust but be soft and creamy inside.

Serves 4–6

300 ml (½ pint) lamb or chicken stock
150 ml (¼ pint) cream
150 ml (¼ pint) milk
1 garlic clove, crushed
1 ½ kg (3 lb) Maris Piper or King Edward potatoes
knob of butter
salt and freshly ground black pepper

Preheat the oven 150°C/300°F/gas 2. Place the stock, cream and milk in a large pan with the garlic and season to taste. Peel and thinly slice the potatoes on a mandolin or using a food processor with an attachment blade.

Add the sliced potatoes to the pan and stir well to ensure that the potatoes are evenly coated. Bring to the boil, then reduce the heat and simmer for about 5 minutes, until the stock mixture has thickened slightly, stirring gently once or twice.

Generously butter an ovenproof dish, then tip in the potato mixture, spreading them out into an even layer. Bake for about 1 hour, until completely tender and lightly golden on top.

To serve, cut into portions and serve at the table to your guests.

Sautéed green beans with olive oil and garlic

Green beans are an excellent vegetable to serve to a crowd. In fact, I'm constantly trying to come up with new ways to use them. This is one of my current favourites. They would also be delicious with two seeded and diced vine tomatoes added to the pan with the beans, but only in the summer when tomatoes are at their best.

Serves 4–6

675 g (1 ½ lb) French green beans, tails removed
3 tablespoons extra virgin olive oil
1 shallot, finely chopped
1 garlic clove, crushed
1 tablespoon chopped fresh flat-leaf parsley
salt and freshly ground black pepper

Plunge the French beans into a large pan of boiling salted water and return to the boil, then boil for a further 2 minutes, until just tender. Drain and refresh under cold running water.

Return the pan to the heat with the olive oil. Tip in the shallot and garlic and sauté for 2–3 minutes, until softened. Add the beans and continue to sauté for a minute or two, until just heated through. Sprinkle in the parsley and toss until well coated. Season to taste.

To serve, transfer to a warmed dish and place on the table so that guests can help themselves.

Roasted balsamic beetroot

This beetroot would also be wonderful served at room temperature as a salad with some orange segments or alongside smoked mackerel with a dollop of horseradish cream.

Serves 4–6

6 large raw beetroot
3 tablespoons balsamic vinegar
1 teaspoon cumin seeds
2 tablespoons olive oil
salt and freshly ground black pepper
roughly chopped fresh flat-leaf parsley, to garnish

Preheat the oven to 200°C/400°F/gas 6. Peel the beetroot and cut each one into 8 wedges. Tip into a roasting tin, then drizzle over the vinegar. Sprinkle the cumin seeds on top and season generously, then drizzle over the oil. Roast for 25–30 minutes, until tender but retaining a bit of bite, turning occasionally.

To serve, transfer to a warmed dish and place on the table so that guests can help themselves.

Mascarpone cheesecake with ginger and lime

This decadent dessert is smooth, silky and rich, perfect for a special lunch as you can make it the day before and keep it in the fridge until needed. If the ginger and lime flavours sound too adventurous for your guests, try using lemon or orange, or even a dash of rum works well.

Serves 6–8

For the base
75 g (3 oz) butter, plus extra for greasing
250 g (9 oz) ginger nut biscuits, crushed

For the filling
1 vanilla pod, split in half and seeds removed
3 x 250 g (9 oz) tubs mascarpone cheese
100 g (4 oz) caster sugar
2 tablespoons cornflour
3 eggs
finely grated rind and juice of 2 limes
½ teaspoon freshly grated root ginger
1 teaspoon finely chopped crystallised stem ginger (from a jar)
strawberries or chunks of fresh pineapple and whipped cream, to serve

Preheat the oven to 160°C/325°F/gas 3. To make the base, lightly butter a 23 cm (9 inch) springform cake tin. Melt the butter in a pan over a gentle heat or in a bowl in the microwave. Add the crushed ginger nut biscuits and mix well. Spread the mixture evenly over the base of the tin, pressing down with the back of a spoon to flatten. Place in the fridge to chill for 10 minutes.

Place a dish of hot water in the oven on the bottom rack; this will stop a skin from forming on the cheesecake. Using the paddle attachment on a food processor, place the vanilla seeds, mascarpone cheese, sugar, cornflour, eggs, lime rind and juice in the mixing bowl. Switch on the machine and beat until smooth, then add both the fresh and stem ginger and mix well to combine. This can also be done in a large bowl with a wooden spoon and a bit of elbow grease.

Pour this mixture into the base-lined cake tin and place on a baking sheet. Bake for 35–45 minutes or until lightly golden. The filling should still be a little wobbly at this stage. Turn off the oven, open the door and carefully run a knife around the cake tin; this prevents the cheesecake from splitting in the middle when cooling. Leave to cool completely; the filling will set as it cools.

To serve, transfer the cheesecake to a cake stand and cut into wedges in front of your guests. Add some fresh fruit to each plate, such as strawberries or pineapple chunks, and a dollop of whipped cream if you're feeling really indulgent.

Rich chocolate cake

I've given two desserts for this magnificent Easter lunch menu. Of course, one would be plenty, but there's something quite special about having a choice, although I normally find that everyone opts for a 'little' taste of each one. Sometimes I fold in a couple of handfuls of white chocolate drops into the mixture just before I pour it into the cake tin to bake.

Serves 6–8

125 g (4 ½ oz) butter, plus extra for greasing
a little plain flour, for dusting
500 g (1 lb 2 oz) plain chocolate, broken into squares (minimum 55% cocoa solids)
6 eggs, separated
75 g (3 oz) caster sugar
150 ml (¼ pint) cream
2 tablespoons dark rum
1 teaspoon vanilla extract
whipped cream and raspberries, to serve

Preheat the oven to 180°C/350°F/gas 4. Butter a 23 cm (9 inch) springform cake tin and lightly flour it, knocking out any excess. Place the butter and chocolate in a heatproof bowl set over a pan of barely simmering water and allow to melt, stirring until smooth. Remove from the pan and set aside to cool a little.

Place the egg yolks and sugar in a bowl. Using an electric mixer or hand whisk, beat until pale and thick. Stir in the cream, then fold in the cooled melted chocolate mixture with the rum and vanilla extract.

Wash the beaters, then whisk the egg whites in a separate bowl until you have achieved soft peaks. Gently fold into the chocolate mixture in three batches until evenly combined. Pour the cake mixture into the prepared cake tin and bake for 25 minutes or until a fine skewer pushed into the centre comes out clean. The cake should be just set with a slight wobble in the middle. Remove the cake from the oven and leave to cool in the tin.

To serve, cut the rich chocolate cake into slices and arrange on plates with a dollop of whipped cream and raspberries.

Christmas
dinner

Roast crown of turkey with sage and onion stuffing

To test if the turkey crown is cooked, pierce the thickest part with a long clean skewer. If the juices run clear, it's ready. If it's a little pink, then return it to the oven and cook a little longer. I prefer to use a free-range or organic bird for this special occasion.

Serves 6–8

4 ½ kg (10 lb) ready-prepared turkey crown (preferably Bronze free-range)
75 g (3 oz) butter, at room temperature
1 garlic clove, crushed
finely grated rind of 1 orange
1 tablespoon chopped fresh flat-leaf parsley
1 teaspoon chopped fresh thyme
4 rindless smoked bacon rashers
1 tablespoon plain flour
300 ml (½ pint) chicken or turkey stock

For the stuffing
75 g (3 oz) butter
1 onion, diced
1 teaspoon chopped fresh sage
50 g (2 oz) pine nuts, toasted
175 g (6 oz) fresh white breadcrumbs
salt and freshly ground black pepper

Glazed loin of bacon (page 131), Brussels sprout, red onion and bacon crumble (page 132), white and sweet potato gratin (page 133) and roasted carrots with garlic and parsley (page 134), to serve

Preheat the oven to 190°C/375°F/gas 5. To make the stuffing, heat a frying pan and add the butter. Add the onion and sage and cook for a few minutes, until softened but not coloured. Add the pine nuts, then stir in the breadcrumbs, mixing well to combine. Season to taste. Wrap the stuffing in buttered tin foil and mould into a large sausage shape. This can be cooked in the oven for 25–30 minutes.

Next, prepare the turkey crown. Cream the butter in a bowl until very soft, then add the crushed garlic, orange rind, parsley and thyme. Beat well, until thoroughly blended. Gently loosen the neck flap away from the breast and pack the flavoured butter right under the skin – this is best done using gloves on your hands. Rub well into the flesh of the turkey, then re-cover the skin and secure with a small skewer or sew with fine twine. Finally, cover the top of the crown with the rashers.

Place the turkey crown in the oven and calculate your time – 20 minutes per 450 g (1 lb) plus 20 minutes, so a joint this size should take 3 hours and 40 minutes. Cover loosely with foil and remove this about 40 minutes before the end of the cooking time. The turkey crown will cook much quicker than a whole turkey, so make sure to keep basting. To check if the turkey is cooked, pierce a fine skewer into the chest part of the crown – the juice should run clear. When cooked, cover with foil to rest and keep warm.

Skim all the fat from the cooking juices, then pour off all but 3 tablespoons of the juices from the roasting tin. Stir the flour into the pan residue and cook, stirring over a low heat, until golden. Gradually pour in the stock, stirring all the time. Bring to the boil and let bubble for 2–3 minutes, until thickened. Season to taste and keep warm.

To serve, carve the turkey crown into slices and arrange on warmed plates with the cooked stuffing, glazed loin of bacon, Brussels sprout, red onion and bacon crumble, white and sweet potato gratin and the roasted carrots with garlic and parsley. Pour the gravy into a warmed gravy jug and hand around separately.

Glazed loin of bacon

The loin of bacon is most often used for bacon rashers but is now becoming widely available in one piece. As it has a lovely even shape, it is perfect for easy carving and is a nice change from the traditional ham, especially served with the redcurrant sauce.

Serves 6–8

1 ½ kg (3 lb) loin of bacon
1 onion, roughly chopped
2 carrots, roughly chopped
2 celery sticks, roughly chopped
a few black peppercorns
1 bay leaf
2 fresh thyme sprigs
1 tablespoon prepared English mustard
1 tablespoon Demerara sugar
2 tablespoons redcurrant jelly
2 tablespoons port
2 tablespoons fresh redcurrants
salt and freshly ground black pepper

Place the bacon joint in a large pan and cover with cold water. Add the onion, carrots, celery, peppercorns, bay leaf and thyme. Bring to the boil, then reduce the heat and simmer gently for 20 minutes per 450 g (1 lb). A joint this size should take no more than 1 hour.

Preheat the oven to 200°C/400°F/gas 6. Remove the cooked bacon joint from the pan and reserve the liquid. Carefully cut the rind from the loin of bacon and score the remaining fat in a criss-cross fashion. Place in a small roasting tin and spread with the mustard and then sprinkle the sugar on top.

Pour 150 ml (¼ pint) of the reserved liquid into the roasting tin (keep the remaining liquid for soup). Place in the oven and roast for 20 minutes, until the fat is nicely glazed and the bacon is completely heated through.

Remove from the oven and transfer to a warmed plate to rest, covered loosely with foil. Place the roasting tin directly on the heat and whisk in the redcurrant jelly, port and redcurrants. Simmer for a couple of minutes, until you have achieved a good, rich consistency. Season to taste.

To serve, carve the rested glazed loin of bacon and arrange on plates with a little of the redcurrant sauce spooned on top.

Brussels sprout, red onion and bacon crumble

If you are not a fan of Brussels sprouts, try using thickly sliced leeks with broccoli or cauliflower instead. This will also make a good vegetarian option for Christmas lunch if you leave out the bacon.

Serves 6–8

675 g (1 ½ oz) Brussels sprouts, trimmed and cut in half
knob of butter
1 large red onion, thinly sliced
2 cooked slices smoked bacon, diced
200 ml (7 fl oz) cream
50 ml (2 fl oz) milk
good pinch freshly grated nutmeg
50 g (2 oz) fresh white breadcrumbs
25 g (1 oz) walnuts, chopped
1 teaspoon chopped fresh flat-leaf parsley
salt and freshly ground black pepper

Preheat the oven to 190°C/375°F/gas 5. Half-fill a pan with water and bring to the boil. Add the Brussels sprouts and simmer for 4–5 minutes, until just tender but not soggy. Drain and refresh under running cold water.

Butter a baking dish and tip in the blanched Brussels sprouts. Scatter over the red onion and bacon. Mix the cream with the milk and nutmeg in a jug and season to taste, then pour over the sprouts. Mix the breadcrumbs with the parsley and walnuts and then sprinkle on top. Place in the oven for 20–25 minutes, until bubbling and golden brown.

To serve, place piping hot directly on the table and allow guests to help themselves.

White and sweet potato gratin

This is a variation on my favourite accompaniment. It's great for Christmas Day, as it can be made in advance and reheated in individual portions on a baking sheet. It also keeps well in a cool oven.

Serves 6–8

600 ml (1 pint) milk
600 ml (1 pint) cream
4 garlic cloves, crushed
good pinch freshly grated nutmeg
1 tablespoon chopped fresh flat-leaf parsley
1 teaspoon chopped fresh thyme
450 g (1 lb) potatoes, peeled
450 g (1 lb) sweet potatoes, peeled (preferably orange-fleshed)
knob of butter
salt and freshly ground white pepper

Preheat the oven to 160°C/325°F/gas 3. Pour the milk and cream into a pan and add the garlic, nutmeg, parsley and thyme. Season to taste and just heat through – do not allow the mixture to boil – then quickly remove from the heat.

Using a mandolin cutter, thinly slice the potatoes and sweet potatoes, being very careful of your fingers, or use the slicing attachment of your food processor, as doing them by hand with a sharp knife can be a very laborious task indeed!

Butter a large ovenproof dish. Arrange a third of the potatoes and sweet potatoes in the bottom and season to taste. Add another third of both types of the potatoes in an even layer. Season to taste. Arrange the rest of the white and sweet potatoes on top in an attractive overlapping layer and pour over the milk mixture.

Cover the gratin with a piece of foil and bake for 1 hour, until cooked through and lightly golden, then remove the foil and return to the oven for another 10 minutes or until the top is bubbling and golden brown.

To serve, divide the white and sweet potato gratin into portions and use as required.

Roasted carrots with garlic and parsley

Roasting vegetables is a fantastic way of feeding a crowd with little effort. These carrots would also be delicious with red onion wedges and a sprinkling of chopped fresh rosemary, or experiment with a selection of similarly prepared root vegetables such as celeriac, parsnips or turnips.

Serves 6–8

500 g (1 lb 2 oz) carrots, scrubbed
2 tablespoons olive oil
caster sugar, to sprinkle
pinch Maldon sea salt
1 garlic bulb, broken into individual cloves
a little balsamic vinegar
2 tablespoons chopped flat-leaf parsley

Preheat the oven to 190°C/375°F/gas 5. Cut the carrots into 1 cm (½ inch) slices on the diagonal and place in a roasting tin. Drizzle with the olive oil and sprinkle lightly with the sugar and salt. Toss well to coat and roast for 15 minutes.

Remove the carrots from the oven and scatter over the unpeeled garlic, tossing until evenly combined. Roast for another 30 minutes, until the carrots and garlic are tender and lightly golden. Drizzle over the balsamic vinegar and scatter over the chopped parsley, again tossing until evenly coated.

To serve, tip into a warmed dish and use as required.

Chocolate chestnut frozen log

This clever dessert can be made well in advance and just needs to be removed from the freezer 1 hour before you are ready to eat. Serve it with any seasonal fruit you fancy, such as mango, blueberries or even orange segments.

Serves 6–8

225 g (8 oz) plain chocolate, broken into squares
150 g (5 oz) butter, cubed and softened
75 g (3 oz) golden caster sugar
25 g (1 oz) cocoa powder
50 g (2 oz) sweetened chestnut purée (from a can)
300 ml (½ pint) cream
4 egg whites
good dash dark rum
whipped cream and raspberries, to serve

Line a 1 ¾ litre (3 pint) loaf tin with cling film. Melt the chocolate and half the butter in a heatproof bowl set over a pan of gently simmering water. Once it has melted, stir with a spatula until smooth and leave to cool slightly.

Place the rest of the butter in a large bowl and add two-thirds of the sugar, then beat with an electric beater or whisk until pale and fluffy. Fold in the cocoa powder and chestnut purée until you have achieved a smooth chocolate-coloured paste.

Whisk the cream in a bowl to soft peaks, but no further. Wash the beaters and dry thoroughly, then whisk the egg whites in a separate bowl to soft peaks and fold in the remaining 25 g (1 oz) of sugar. Then fold in the cooled melted chocolate mixture, followed by the cocoa chestnut paste. Fold in the whipped cream with the rum, then finally, fold in the meringue. Pour into the prepared loaf tin, then gently bang on a surface to settle. Freeze until solid.

To serve, remove from the freezer about 1 hour before you are ready to eat, then turn out onto a flat plate and carefully peel away the cling film. Cut into slices and arrange on plates with the whipped cream and raspberries.

Coconut and mango meringue pie

As this pastry is so short, it is in danger of breaking up when you are trying to roll it out. If this happens, try coarsely grating it directly into the tin and then quickly pressing the pastry up the sides and into the shape of the tin. No one will ever know the difference – promise!

Serves 6–8

For the pastry
100 g (4 oz) butter, chilled and diced, plus extra for greasing
175 g (6 oz) plain flour, plus extra for dusting
pinch salt
50 g (2 oz) caster sugar
1 egg yolk
½ tablespoon cream

For the filling
finely grated rind and juice of 3 limes
175 g (6 oz) caster sugar
300 ml (½ pint) coconut milk
2 tablespoons cornflour
1 ripe mango, peeled, stoned and diced or 400 g (14 oz) can mango slices in syrup, drained
4 egg yolks
50 g (2 oz) butter, softened

For the meringue
2 egg whites
100 g (4 oz) caster sugar
whipped cream, to serve

To make the pastry, place the butter, flour, salt and sugar into a food processor and blend for 20 seconds. Add the egg yolk and cream and blend again, until the dough just comes together. Do not over-work or the pastry will be tough. Wrap in cling film and chill for 1 hour.

Thinly roll out the pastry on a lightly floured board and use to line a buttered 20 cm (8 inch) loose-bottomed flan tin. Prick the base with a fork and then chill for about 20 minutes.

Preheat the oven to 200°C/400°F/gas 6. Line the pastry case with tin foil and a thin layer of baking beans or dried pulses. Bake for 15–20 minutes, until golden. Reduce the oven temperature to 180°C/350°F/gas 4. Remove the pastry case from the oven and carefully remove the foil, then return to the oven for 3–5 minutes, until lightly golden.

To make the filling, place the lime rind and juice in a pan with the sugar and coconut milk, then heat gently until the sugar dissolves, stirring occasionally. Mix the cornflour in a small bowl with 2 tablespoons of cold water, then stir into the coconut mixture. Bring to the boil and cook for 2 minutes, until thickened, stirring continuously. Remove from the heat and fold in the mango, then leave to cool slightly. Finally, beat in the egg yolks and butter. Pour into the pastry case and leave to cool completely.

To make the meringue, place the egg whites in a large bowl and whisk into soft peaks, then gradually whisk in the sugar a spoonful at a time to make a stiff, glossy meringue. Spoon on top of the filling, spreading it out to make sure it makes a good seal with the pastry edge. Swirl the top of the meringue with the tip of a knife and bake for 15 minutes, until lightly golden. Carefully remove the tart from the tin and leave to cool slightly.

To serve, cut into slices and arrange on plates with whipped cream.

The best-ever Irish coffee

A little indulgence is a wonderful thing and it doesn't come much better than this, a dark, luxurious Irish coffee with a couple of extra shots of liqueur, topped with lightly whipped cream. Make them to order and watch your guests enjoy every sip.

Serves 6-8

350 ml (12 fl oz) cream, well chilled
50 g (2 oz) sugar
120 ml (4 fl oz) whiskey
120 ml (4 fl oz) Bailey's Irish cream
120 ml (4 fl oz) Kahlúa (coffee liqueur)
1.2 litres (2 pints) freshly brewed espresso coffee (piping hot)
pinch freshly grated nutmeg

Heat a small heavy-based frying pan over a medium heat. Meanwhile, place the cream in a bowl and lightly whip, then chill until needed.

Sprinkle the sugar over the base of the frying pan and allow it to caramelise without stirring. Pour in the whiskey and quickly flambé, then stir in the Bailey's and Kahlúa and cook over a low heat until smooth, stirring occasionally.

Pour the liqueur mixture into hefty, thick-stemmed glasses and pour in the coffee. Then, over the back of a spoon, carefully pour a layer of the lightly whipped cream on top.

To serve, add a tiny grating of nutmeg to each glass.

Frangipane mince pies

I've my Auntie Maureen to thank for this brilliant recipe. I always freeze a large batch, as I find them very handy to have over the Christmas period. For mincemeat that will keep well, use a firm, hard type of eating apple; juicy apples, such as Bramleys, may make the mixture too moist. If time allows, leave it to stand for 2 days, then stir well and put into sterilised jars and cover (as for jam). Allow at least 2 weeks to mature before using, and up to 1 year is fine.

Makes about 40

For the mincemeat
350 g (12 oz) eating apples
225 g (8 oz) raisins
225 g (8 oz) sultanas
225 g (8 oz) currants
100 g (4 oz) mixed peel (preferably homemade)
175 g (6 oz) blanched almonds, chopped
175 g (6 oz) dark muscovado sugar
finely grated rind of 1 orange
finely grated rind of 1 lemon
½ teaspoon freshly grated or ground nutmeg
1 teaspoon ground cinnamon
½ teaspoon ground cloves
½ teaspoon salt
225 g (8 oz) butter
300 ml (½ pint) whiskey

For the pastry
100 g (4 oz) butter, chilled and diced, plus extra for greasing
175 g (6 oz) plain flour, plus extra for dusting
pinch salt
50 g (2 oz) caster sugar
1 egg yolk
½ tablespoon cream

For the almond filling
225 g (8 oz) butter

225 g (8 oz) icing sugar
50 g (2 oz) plain flour
225 g (8 oz) ground almonds
4 eggs
large pinch ground cinnamon
1 vanilla pod, halved and seeds scraped out
icing sugar, to dust
whipped cream, to serve (optional)

To make the mincemeat, peel and core the apples, then coarsely grate. Place in a large bowl with the raisins, sultanas, currants, mixed peel, almonds, sugar, orange and lemon rind, spices and salt. Melt the butter in the microwave or in a small pan and allow to cool slightly, then stir into the fruit mixture with the whiskey. Leave for 2 days to allow the flavours to develop, then pack into sterilised dry jars, seal and store in a cool, dark place.

To make the pastry, place the butter, flour, salt and sugar into a food processor and blend for 20 seconds. Add the egg yolk and cream and blend again, until the dough just comes together. Do not over-work or the pastry will be tough. Wrap in cling film and chill for 1 hour.

To make the almond filling, using an electric beater, cream the butter and icing sugar together in a large bowl until pale and fluffy. Fold in the flour and ground almonds and then gradually beat in the eggs, cinnamon and vanilla seeds. Beat for 5 minutes, until light and fluffy.

Roll out the pastry on a lightly floured surface. Cut out 40 rounds with a 7 ½ cm (3 inch) fluted cutter. Line 6 cm (2 ½ inch) patty tins with the pastry rounds and fill with the mincemeat. Spoon the almond filling on top to cover the mincemeat completely and place in the oven to bake for 15–18 minutes, until cooked through and lightly golden. Leave to cool in the tins for 5 minutes, then transfer to a wire rack to cool completely.

To serve, arrange on plates and dust with icing sugar. Add a small dollop of whipped cream to each plate.

Al Fresco
lunch

Long Island iced tea

*This has to be the ultimate thirst quencher for those long, hot summer days.
It definitely packs a serious alcohol punch, so go easy on it. I'd probably only
serve one to each guest to get everyone relaxed and in the party mood.*

Serves 6

juice of 3 lemons
4 tablespoons icing sugar
120 ml (4 fl oz) light rum
120 ml (4 fl oz) tequila
120 ml (4 fl oz) gin
120 ml (4 fl oz) vodka
4 tablespoons Cointreau or another orange-flavoured liqueur
about 225 g (8 oz) ice cubes
600 ml (1 pint) Coca-Cola, well chilled
lemon slices and fresh mint sprigs, to decorate

Place the lemon juice and icing sugar into a tall jug and stir until the sugar has
dissolved. Measure in the rum, tequila, gin, vodka and Cointreau, stirring to combine.

Fill tall glasses with ice and pour over the boozy mixture, then top each one up
with Coca-Cola. Decorate with lemon slices and mint sprigs before serving.

Variations

Tropical Pimm's

Thread cubes of fresh pineapple and lime wedges onto bamboo skewers, then
stick in tall glasses with fresh mint sprigs and plenty of ice. Mix a bottle of Pimm's
with 750 ml (1 ¼ pints) of traditional ginger beer in a large jug, then pour into the
glasses to serve.

Sangria

Mix the juice of 2 lemons with 4 tablespoons of caster sugar in a tall jug until
dissolved, then fill with a sliced orange and lemon and plenty of ice. Add 300 ml
(½ pint) of fruity red wine and 120 ml (4 fl oz) of brandy. Pour in 300 ml (½ pint)
of sparkling mineral water and stir to combine. Pour into tall glasses to serve.

Grilled chicken salad with roasted garlic and basil dressing

This is a great main course salad. The simple marinade for the chicken does everything you could wish for and helps to keep it moist during cooking. If you want to cook the chicken on a charcoal barbecue, light it 30 minutes before you want to start cooking. If using a gas barbecue, light it 10 minutes beforehand.

Serves 4–6

RTÉ **GUIDE**

READER TESTED

4 skinless chicken breast fillets
2 heads of romaine lettuce, washed and roughly cut

For the marinade
1 tablespoon dark soy sauce
1 tablespoon clear honey
1 garlic clove, crushed
1 tablespoon sweet chilli sauce

For the dressing
1 garlic clove, unpeeled
6 tablespoons olive oil
1 tablespoon red wine vinegar
1 tablespoon balsamic vinegar
½ teaspoon Dijon mustard
1 small red onion, very finely diced
1 tablespoon chopped fresh basil
salt and freshly ground black pepper

To make the marinade, place the soy sauce in a shallow non-metallic dish with the honey, garlic and sweet chilli sauce. Mix well to combine. Make three shallow diagonal slashes on top of each chicken breast and place them in the dish, turning to coat. Cover with cling film and leave to marinade in the fridge for at least 6 hours or overnight if time allows.

Preheat the grill. Place the garlic clove in a small pan with the olive oil and heat gently for 10–12 minutes, until the garlic is cooked through but not coloured. Leave to cool completely, then mash up the softened garlic with a fork. Set aside until you want to finish making the dressing.

Place the chicken on a grill rack and cook under the grill for 7–8 minutes on each side, until cooked through, brushing regularly with any remaining excess marinade. Remove from the heat and leave to cool slightly, then cut into slices.

To finish making the dressing, place the garlic olive oil in a jam jar with the vinegars, mustard, red onion and basil. Season to taste, then place the lid on top and shake well, until thick and creamy.

To serve, arrange the lettuce leaves around bowls or plates, scatter the chicken over the salad and drizzle the dressing over.

Three-tomato salad with basil

This tomato salad is visually enticing, and the different varieties of tomatoes each have their own individual textures and flavours. It takes very little time to prepare and looks fantastic on the table.

Serves 4–6

2 beef tomatoes, thinly sliced
4 ripe tomatoes, cut into wedges
100 g (4 oz) sun-gold or baby plum cherry tomatoes, halved
1 shallot, thinly sliced
handful fresh basil leaves, shredded

For the dressing
1 tablespoon balsamic vinegar
½ teaspoon clear honey
pinch salt
4 tablespoons extra virgin olive oil
1 small garlic clove, crushed
salt and freshly ground black pepper

To make the dressing, place the vinegar in a screw-top jar and add the honey and a good pinch of salt, then shake until the salt has dissolved. Add the oil to the jar with the garlic and shake again until you have formed a thick emulsion. Season to taste and chill until needed.

To serve, arrange the beef tomatoes in a single layer on the base of a large plate, then scatter over the tomato wedges and finish with a pile of the cherry tomatoes. Sprinkle over the shallot and basil and then drizzle the balsamic and honey dressing on top. Add a good grinding of pepper and leave at room temperature for up to 1 hour.

Field mushrooms with spinach, blue cheese and caramelised red onion

This makes a lovely accompaniment to the grilled chicken salad (page 146) or to have as a vegetarian alternative for your lunch. Otherwise use as a simple starter and replace the blue cheese with goat's cheese and serve on a bed of salad drizzled with a little a pesto. Try to choose deep field mushrooms with curled-up edges so that they hold the filling in place.

Serves 4–6

4 tablespoons olive oil
450 g (1 lb) spinach, washed and thick stalks removed
2 garlic cloves, crushed
1 red onion, finely diced
6 baby vine tomatoes, cut in half
25 g (1 oz) toasted pine nuts or walnuts
8 large field mushrooms, wiped clean (evenly sized)
100 g (4 oz) mild blue cheese, diced (such as Cashel blue)
salt and freshly ground black pepper

Preheat the oven to 230°C/450°F/gas 8. Heat 1 tablespoon of the olive oil in a large pan, add the spinach and stir-fry over a large heat until just wilted. Tip out onto a layer of kitchen paper to absorb the excess liquid. Place the spinach on a chopping board and roughly chop.

Add another tablespoon of olive oil to the pan, then add the garlic and red onion. Cook for 5 minutes, until soft, stirring occasionally. Stir in the vine tomatoes and allow to just warm through. Tip in the toasted pine nuts or walnuts with the chopped spinach and season to taste.

Remove the stalks from the mushrooms and keep for soup or discard. Brush with the remaining olive oil and place in a baking tin, gill side up. Season generously and bake for 5 minutes, then remove and spoon the spinach mixture on top.

Scatter over the blue cheese and place back in the oven for another 6–10 minutes, until the mushrooms are completely tender and the cheese has melted and is golden brown.

To serve, arrange on a large platter and allow guests to help themselves.

New potato salad

Everyone loves potatoes and this is a great way of serving them on a warm summer's day. I often cook the potatoes just before people arrive – that way it's lovely and fresh when you're serving it.

Serves 4–6

900 g (2 lb) small, waxy new potatoes, scraped or scrubbed
2 teaspoons white wine vinegar
2 tablespoons light olive oil
4 tablespoons mayonnaise
2 tablespoons crème fraîche
1 bunch spring onions, trimmed and thinly sliced
2 tablespoons chopped fresh dill
2 tablespoons chopped fresh flat-leaf parsley
salt and freshly ground black pepper

If necessary, cut the potatoes into 2 ½ cm (1 inch) chunks. Place in a pan of salted water, bring to the boil and cook for 12–15 minutes or until tender. This will depend on your potatoes, so keep an eye on them.

Meanwhile, whisk together the white wine vinegar in a small bowl with the olive oil and season to taste. Drain the potatoes well, transfer to a serving bowl and gently stir in the vinegar and olive oil mixture. Leave to cool completely.

Stir the mayonnaise and crème fraîche together in a small bowl and stir into the potatoes with the spring onions, dill and parsley. Season to taste.

To serve, either use immediately or cover with cling film and chill until needed. This will keep very well in the fridge for up to 24 hours.

Watermelon and lime ice lollies

Refreshing and aromatic, these lollies are excellent thirst quenchers, almost like a frozen cocktail on a stick. Pass them around at the end of lunch to help refresh and cleanse the palette. Obviously you can omit the alcohol if serving them to children or designated drivers.

Serves 6–8

75 g (3 oz) caster sugar
85 ml (3 fl oz) water
finely pared rind of 2 limes, all white pith removed
275 g (10 oz) wedge fresh watermelon
2 tablespoons vodka (optional)
juice of 1 lime

Place the sugar in a pan and pour in the water. Place over a very gentle heat and allow the sugar to dissolve, without boiling, until completely clear. Then bring the syrup to the boil and boil for 4–5 minutes or until it is 102°C/215°F (short thread stage). Remove from the heat and place the pan in a basin filled with cold water to cool the syrup down slightly. Stir in the lime rind and allow to chill. You should have about 50 ml (2 fl oz) of the lime sugar syrup in total.

Meanwhile, cut the watermelon flesh away from the skin and cut into chunks, picking out and discarding the seeds. Place in a food processor and process for 1–2 minutes or until the flesh has liquefied. Strain through a sieve into a large jug and stir in the lime sugar syrup with the vodka, if using, and the lime juice. Pour the mixture into ice lolly moulds; the amount you make will depend on the size of your moulds. Place in the freezer for 4–6 hours or until the lollies are completely frozen.

To serve, quickly dip the moulds into boiling hot water to remove the lollies and hand around to your guests.

Variations

Pineapple and mint

Use a small pineapple that has been peeled, cored and roughly chopped instead of the watermelon and add a good handful of mint leaves when blitzing in the food processor. Replace the vodka with light rum.

Mango and coconut

Replace the watermelon with 1 large ripe mango that has been peeled and the flesh cut away from the stone. Add 5 tablespoons of coconut milk instead of the lime juice and vodka.

Chocolate pots with shortbread

These chocolate pots are rich, light and fluffy and are just perfect served with the shortbread on the side. Good-quality chocolate makes all the difference, so try and get chocolate with a minimum of 50% cocoa solids. The recipe for the shortbread makes more biscuits than you'll need, so serve with coffee or give as a gift as guests are going home.

Serves 6

For the chocolate pots
450 ml (¾ pint) cream
75 g (3 oz) golden caster sugar
1 teaspoon vanilla extract
250 g (9 oz) plain chocolate, broken into squares (or buttons)
3 tablespoons Bailey's Irish cream
small pinch salt
1 large egg, beaten

For the shortbread
40 g (1 ½ oz) icing sugar, plus extra for dusting
250 g (9 oz) butter, at room temperature
50 g (2 oz) cornflour
175 g (6 oz) plain flour
1 teaspoon vanilla extract
pinch salt
whipped cream and grated plain chocolate, to decorate

To make the shortbread, sift the icing sugar into a bowl and add the butter, then beat together with an electric beater until just combined. Sift the cornflour and plain flour into a separate bowl.

Add the vanilla extract to the butter and sugar mixture, then tip in the sifted flour and cornflour mixture with the salt. Mix to form a smooth dough. Mould and shape into a log, then wrap in cling film and place in the fridge for at least 30 minutes (or overnight is fine).

Preheat the oven to 180°C/350°F/gas 4. Remove the shortbread dough from the fridge and cut into 1 cm (½ inch) slices, then cut into shapes with a 5 cm (2 inch) fluted edge. Re-roll the excess dough and repeat until the dough is used up. Place on a baking sheet lined with non-stick parchment paper. Bake for 8–10 minutes, until golden brown. Leave to cool on a wire rack, then dust with icing sugar. These will keep well for up to 2 days stored in an airtight container.

To make the chocolate pots, pour the cream into a small pan and add the sugar and vanilla extract. Warm gently for 3–4 minutes, stirring occasionally, but do not allow to boil. Remove from the heat and stir in the chocolate until melted and the mixture is very smooth, then whisk in the Bailey's with the salt and egg until well combined.

Pour the chocolate mixture into teacups or small ramekins, gently tapping until the tops are smooth. Cover loosely with foil or cling film, then leave somewhere cold (not the fridge) for 4 hours or until set. Alternatively, chill overnight and allow to come back to room temperature before serving.

To serve, put the teacups or ramekins onto saucers, decorate with some whipped cream and grated chocolate and serve with shortbread.

After Eight
occasions

St Valentine's
dinner

Roast salmon and goat's cheese salad

There are no hard and fast rules for this salad, so don't be afraid to play around with a few different salad ingredients depending on what you like. Experiment with the wide range of goat's cheeses that are now available from your local supermarkets, and don't forget to have a look at what's on the delicatessen counter.

Serves 2

1 small baguette, cut into 1 cm (½ inch) slices
olive oil, for brushing
2 x 100 g (4 oz) salmon fillets, scaled (preferably organic)
50 g (2 oz) fresh salad leaves, such as a mixture of rocket, watercress and baby spinach
4 fresh mint leaves, torn
1 teaspoon snipped fresh chives
5 cm (2 inch) piece cucumber, peeled, halved, seeds removed and thinly sliced
50 g (2 oz) cooked baby beetroot, thinly sliced
6 vine cherry tomatoes, cut in half
50 g (2 oz) medium soft goat's cheese

For the dressing
3 tablespoons extra virgin olive oil
1 tablespoon red wine vinegar
pinch caster sugar
½ teaspoon Dijon mustard
salt and freshly ground black pepper

Preheat the oven to 200°C/400°F/gas 6. Arrange the bread slices on a baking sheet, brush lightly with olive oil and bake for 10 minutes, until golden brown. Leave to cool.

Arrange the salmon fillets in a small baking tin, then brush with a little olive oil and season to taste. Bake for 8–10 minutes, until just cooked through and lightly golden. Leave to cool, then roughly flake the flesh, discarding any bones and the skin.

To serve, arrange the salad leaves on plates and scatter the mint, chives and cucumber on top with the beetroot and cherry tomatoes. Divide the salmon flakes among the plates and crumble over the goat's cheese. Cover with cling film and chill until needed.

To make the dressing, place the olive oil in a screw-top jar with the vinegar, sugar, mustard and seasoning, then shake to form an emulsion. Set aside until needed.

To serve, remove the salads from the fridge 1 hour before you want to eat to allow them to come back to room temperature. Drizzle over the dressing and serve with the toasted baguette.

Seared fillet steak with cracked black pepper sauce

For me, there's nothing nicer for a romantic dinner than a tender steak, garnished with a huge pile of these crispy onion rings – delicious. I always choose Irish beef, as I'm confident of the traceability from farm to plate. The accompanying pepper sauce can be made up to 1 week in advance and kept covered in the fridge until you are ready to serve. Remember the motto: everything in moderation, and a little in excess...

Serves 2

sunflower oil, for deep-frying
large knob butter
1 small shallot, finely chopped
75 g (3 oz) button mushrooms, sliced
50 ml (2 fl oz) whiskey
½ teaspoon cracked black pepper
85 ml (3 fl oz) beef stock
85 ml (3 fl oz) cream
1 tablespoon olive oil
2 x 150 g (5 oz) fillet steaks
1 large Spanish onion
25 g (1 oz) plain flour
salt and freshly ground black pepper
shoestring chips (page 163) and green bean and rocket salad (page 164), to serve

Preheat the oven to 200°C/400°F/gas 6 and heat a deep-fat fryer to 180°C/350°F or 5 cm (2 inches) of the sunflower oil in a wok or deep-sided sauté pan to make the onion rings.

To make the cracked black pepper sauce, heat a pan and add the butter. Once it's melted and foaming, add the shallot and mushrooms. Cook for 2–3 minutes, until the shallot has softened and the mushrooms are tender, tossing the pan occasionally.

Pour the whiskey into the mushroom mixture and season with the cracked black pepper. To burn off some of the harsh alcoholic taste of the whiskey, flame it off a little by tipping the edge of the pan over the flames very carefully. When it burns off, stir in the stock and slowly add the cream. Reduce for about 5 minutes, until you have achieved a sauce consistency, stirring occasionally, then season to taste. Set aside and keep warm until needed.

Heat the olive oil in a heavy-based ovenproof frying pan over a high heat. Season the steaks with plenty of black pepper and cook for 1 minute on each side to seal in the juices, then transfer to the oven and cook the steak uncovered for another 5–10 minutes, turning once, depending on how rare you like your meat.

Meanwhile, make the onion rings. Peel the onion and slice into 1 cm (½ inch) slices, then separate into rings. Sprinkle with a pinch of salt and leave to stand for 2–3 minutes, then toss in the flour. Shake off the excess and deep-fry for 2–3 minutes, until crisp and golden brown. Drain well on kitchen paper and keep warm.

Transfer the cooked steak to warmed plates, season with salt and set aside in a warm place to rest while you assemble the dish. Pour any juices that run off the meat into your pepper sauce for added flavour.

To serve, pile the crispy onion rings on top of the rested steaks and drizzle around the cracked black pepper sauce. Serve the shoestring chips and green bean and rocket salad in separate bowls.

Shoestring chips

These make an excellent accompaniment to my seared fillet steak with cracked black pepper sauce (see page 161) or just about anything, really. You need a mandolin to prepare the potatoes, as it is extremely difficult to get them right by hand. Chinese mandolins have come down in price in recent years and you should be able to pick one up for a reasonable price.

Serves 2

sunflower oil, for deep-frying
450 g (1 lb) large potatoes
good pinch salt

Heat the sunflower oil to 190°C/375°F in a deep-fat fryer or large pan. Use a cooking thermometer if necessary.

While the oil is heating, prepare the potatoes. Peel the potatoes, then, using the mandolin, cut them into long, thin strips so they resemble shoestrings (fine julienne).

Place the potatoes in a large bowl and set aside for 3–5 minutes, until the starch begins to leak from the potatoes and the mixture starts to look sticky.

Deep-fry the potatoes for 3–4 minutes, until golden brown. Drain on plenty of kitchen paper and season to taste.

To serve, pile the shoestring potatoes into a warmed bowl and season with the salt.

Green bean and rocket salad

This very simple salad needs little or no preparation but adds a lovely fresh crunch to the seared fillet steak with cracked black pepper sauce (see page 161). It can be served hot or at room temperature, depending on what suits.

Serves 2

225 g (8 oz) French beans, tails removed
1 tablespoon extra virgin olive oil
1 small shallot, finely sliced
1 small garlic clove, crushed
1 teaspoon chopped fresh flat-leaf parsley
pinch salt
25 g (1 oz) rocket

Plunge the French beans into a large pan of boiling salted water. Blanch for 2 minutes, until just tender, then drain and refresh under cold running water.

Place the pan back on the heat. Add the olive oil, shallot and garlic and sauté for 1–2 minutes, then add the blanched French beans and cook for another 2 minutes, tossing the pan occasionally. Scatter over the parsley, tossing to combine, and season with the salt.

To serve, arrange the rocket on a plate and spoon the French bean mixture on top.

Passion fruit mousse with lemon sablés

This passion fruit mousse is the perfect way to end a special meal. It can be made well in advance and kept in the fridge until needed. The delicious biscuits are crisp, yet melt in the mouth and are perfect for dipping. If you haven't got a heart-shaped cutter, try doing them free hand – after all, it's the thought that counts...

Serves 2

finely grated rind of 2 lemons
50 g (2 oz) caster sugar
3 passion fruit, halved and pulp scooped out
2 eggs, separated
40 g (1 ½ oz) butter, diced and chilled
6 raspberries

For the lemon sablés
50 g (2 oz) plain flour, plus extra for dusting
25 g (1 oz) icing sugar, plus extra for dusting
finely grated rind of 1 lemon
50 g (2 oz) butter, at room temperature
1 egg yolk

To make the lemon sablés, sift the flour and icing sugar into a bowl. Stir in the lemon rind, then add the butter and egg yolk. Beat well to form a soft dough. Wrap in cling film and chill for at least 30 minutes (up to 3 days is fine).

Preheat the oven to 190°C/375°F/gas 5. Roll out the dough on a lightly floured surface to a 3 mm (⅛ inch) thickness. Stamp out heart shapes or 2 ½ cm (1 inch) rounds using a biscuit cutter, then transfer to baking sheets lined with non-stick parchment paper. Bake for 8–10 minutes, until crisp and lightly golden.

To make the passion fruit mousse, place the lemon rind in a heatproof bowl with half of the sugar, the pulp from 2 of the passion fruit and the egg yolks. Set over a pan of simmering water and cook over a low heat for 8–10 minutes, until the

mixture coats the back of a spoon, stirring occasionally. Whisk in the butter a little at a time until smooth and shiny. Remove from heat and leave to cool.

Whisk the egg whites in a separate bowl until soft peaks form, then add the remaining sugar, a tablespoon at a time, until stiff and shiny. Fold half of the egg whites into the cooled passion fruit mixture using a slotted spoon, then fold in the remainder. Divide among Martini glasses and chill for at least 2 hours or overnight is fine, covered with cling film.

To serve, arrange the glasses on plates and decorate each glass with the pulp from half a passion fruit and the raspberries. Place a couple of the lemon sablés on the side for dipping. Yum.

Anniversary
dinner

Coconut spiced prawn skewers

These are so easy to prepare, yet so colourful and visually appetising. Buy large raw tiger prawns, and if you are buying them frozen, you will need to buy a few more, as they lose quite a lot of their weight when they defrost. About 900 g (2 lb) will give you 675 g (1 ½ lb) once they have thawed out.

Serves 4–6

RTÉ **GUIDE**

READER TESTED

675 g (1 ½ lb) raw headless tiger prawns
1 lemon grass stalk
4 limes
2 garlic cloves, finely chopped
160 ml (5 ½ fl oz) can coconut cream
6 tablespoons light soy sauce
2 teaspoons palm or light muscovado sugar

For the dipping sauce
1 baby or ½ cucumber
85 ml (3 fl oz) rice wine or white wine vinegar
25 g (1 oz) caster sugar
1 red bird's eye chilli, seeded and finely chopped
1 tablespoon chopped roasted peanuts

Soak twelve 15 cm (6 inch) bamboo skewers in a shallow dish of cold water for at least 30 minutes.

Peel the prawns, if necessary, leaving the last tail segment in place. Remove the tough outer leaves from the stalk of lemon grass and finely chop the tender core. Finely grate the rind from one of the limes and squeeze out the juice. Cut the remaining limes into small wedges.

Put the lemon grass, lime rind, lime juice, garlic, coconut cream, soy sauce and sugar into a non-metallic dish. Add the prawns, mix together well and set aside to marinate at room temperature for 15 minutes or for up to 2 hours in the fridge.

To make the dipping sauce, cut the cucumber in half and scoop out the seeds with a teaspoon. Cut the remaining cucumber into very small dice and place in a bowl. Mix in the vinegar, sugar and chilli until the sugar has dissolved and spoon into small serving bowls. Sprinkle over peanuts.

Preheat a griddle pan or barbecue. Thread four prawns onto each skewer, alternating with the lime wedges. Cook the skewers for about 1 minute on each side or until just cooked through.

To serve, arrange on plates with the bowls of dipping sauce and garnish with the remaining lime wedges.

Glazed five-spice duck breasts

This is a fantastic way of jazzing up ready-prepared duck breasts, as there is no preparation at all involved. They are best served slightly pink in the centre, but just cook them for a bit longer if you prefer them more well done.

Serves 4–6

4–6 x 175 g (6 oz) Peking duck breasts (such as Thornhill)
1 teaspoon Chinese five-spice powder
2 tablespoons clear honey
4 tablespoons kecap manis (sweet soy sauce)
2 tablespoons balsamic vinegar
1 red chilli, seeded and finely chopped
purple sprouting broccoli with lemon and chilli (page 174) and fragrant rice with sizzling spiced oil (page 175), to serve

Lightly score the skin of each duck breast into a diamond pattern with the tip of a sharp knife, taking care not to cut through to the meat.

Heat a large heavy-based frying pan (you may need two depending on their size) until it is quite hot. Add the duck breasts, skin side down, lower the heat to medium and cook for about 3–4 minutes, until the skin is crisp and golden brown.

Turn the breasts over and cook them for another 5 minutes, or a little longer if you don't like your duck too pink. Meanwhile, mix together the five-spice powder, honey, kecap manis, balsamic vinegar and chilli in a small bowl.

Pour away all of the excess fat from the pan. Add the honey mixture and leave it to bubble away, turning the duck breasts occasionally for 1–2 minutes, until they are nicely glazed. Remove from the heat and leave to rest in a warm place for a couple of minutes.

To serve, arrange the purple sprouting broccoli with lemon and chilli on warmed plates. Slice each duck breast on the diagonal and carefully lift on top of the broccoli. Spoon over any remaining glaze. Have a separate dish of the fragrant rice with sizzling spiced oil to hand around.

Purple sprouting broccoli with lemon and chilli

If you have trouble getting hold of purple sprouting broccoli, try using the long-stemmed variety. Courgettes also work well cooked like this – simply cut them into batons first. I devised this to be served with the glazed five-spice duck breasts (see page 173), but it would also be delicious served with a pan-fried piece of salmon or chicken.

Serves 4–6

275 g (10 oz) purple sprouting broccoli
2 tablespoons sunflower oil
2 garlic cloves, thinly sliced
1 red chilli, seeded and thinly sliced
finely grated rind and juice of ½ lemon
salt and freshly ground black pepper

Trim the broccoli stems, then cut into long florets, leaving a good length of stalk on each piece. Cook the broccoli in a pan of boiling water for 2 minutes, then drain thoroughly.

Heat the sunflower oil in a wok or non-stick frying pan and cook the garlic for a few seconds. Add the blanched broccoli with the chilli and stir fry for 2–3 minutes, until the broccoli is tender but still firm. Add the lemon rind and juice and season to taste, tossing well to combine.

To serve, use as required.

Fragrant rice with sizzling spiced oil

This recipe uses basmati rice, the undisputed queen of rice. It actually triples in length as it cooks and fills the house with the most heavenly scent, then it has sizzling hot oil poured over just before it's served.

Serves 4–6

350 g (12 oz) basmati rice, well rinsed
600 ml (1 pint) boiling water
1 bay leaf
½ cinnamon stick
2 whole cloves
pinch salt

For the spiced oil
3 tablespoons sunflower oil
1 tablespoon black mustard seeds
2 teaspoons cumin seeds
chopped fresh coriander, to garnish

Wash the rice in numerous changes of cold water until the water runs relatively clear. Cover with more cold water and leave to soak for 5 minutes, then drain well.

Place the rinsed rice into a pan with the boiling water. Add the bay leaf, cinnamon, cloves and salt, stirring to combine, and quickly bring to the boil. Stir once, cover with a tight-fitting lid and cook over a low heat for 12 minutes, until tender.

Once the rice is cooked, make the spiced oil. Heat the oil in a small pan until it is fairly hot (almost but not quite smoking). Tip the cooked rice into a warmed dish.

To serve, add the mustard and cumin seeds to the heated oil. Once they start to pop and smell fragrant, immediately tip over the rice. Garnish with the coriander.

Fresh pineapple with lime sorbet

Juicy limes are very important for this sorbet. Choose limes that feel heavier in the hand and that give a little when squeezed. Thin-skinned limes yield the most juice, as do slightly older limes, recognised by their muddy yellow colour. This discoloration is caused by dehydration, which actually increases the juice content inside, so it's often worth popping down to the market and seeking out old stock – at a knocked down price, of course!

Serves 4–6

3 limes
250 g (9 oz) caster sugar
10 good-quality tea bags (orange pekoe Ceylon work particularly well)
1 large ripe pineapple

To make the syrup for the sorbet, finely grate the rind from the limes and squeeze out the juice. Set aside.

Place 250 g (9 oz) of the sugar in a pan with 1 litre (1 ¾ pints) of water and cook over a low heat until dissolved, then boil fast for 2–3 minutes. Remove from the heat, pour into a large bowl and set aside, leaving 150 ml (¼ pint) of the syrup behind in the pan. Add the lime rind and simmer for about 15 minutes, until completely tender, stirring occasionally and being careful not to let it boil away and burn. Reserve 4 tablespoons to use for the pineapple in a separate small bowl.

Place 300 ml (½ pint) of water in a separate pan with the tea bags and bring to the boil, then remove from the heat and set aside for 3–5 minutes to infuse. Taste after 3 minutes – if you're happy with the flavour, then remove the tea bags. If you want it a little stronger, infuse the tea bags for a few more minutes – just don't allow the tea to infuse for too long or it will go bitter. Strain into a jug, discarding the tea bags.

Stir the lime juice into the reserved sugar syrup in the large bowl. Add the rind mixture and the tea infusion and stir to combine. It's important to taste at this stage – you may want to add extra sugar or lime juice accordingly – then leave to cool completely. Place into an ice cream/sorbet machine and churn according to manufacturer's instructions – you should get 1.2 litres (2 pints) of sorbet in total.

Slice the top and bottom off the pineapple, sit it upright on a board and slice away the skin and all the little brown 'eyes'. Cut the fruit lengthways into quarters, then cut away about 2 ½ cm (1 inch) of the sharper edges of each wedge to remove the core, which can be quite woody. Now cut the pineapple across each wedge into thin slices and arrange on a large plate. Cover with cling film and chill in the fridge until needed.

To serve, arrange the pineapple on plates and drizzle over the reserved lime syrup. Add a couple of scoops of the lime sorbet to each one.

Late Late
Toy Show

Crunchy and sweet spiced nuts

These crunchy spiced nuts are an excellent nibble. I like to use a mixture of blanched almonds, raw cashew nuts and pecan halves, but any mixed nut selection would work well. Make up to 3 days in advance, leave to cool completely and store in an airtight container at room temperature.

Serves 4–6

50 g (2 oz) unsalted butter
450 g (1 lb) mixed nuts
2 garlic cloves, crushed
2 teaspoons garam masala
¼ teaspoon ground paprika
¼ teaspoon ground cumin
1 teaspoon chilli powder
2 teaspoons salt
2 egg whites
2 tablespoons light muscovado sugar

Preheat the oven to 180°C/350°F/gas 4. Melt the butter in a bowl in the microwave or in a pan. Add the nuts and garlic and stir to combine, then spread out in a large roasting tin.

Mix the garam masala, paprika, cumin, chilli powder and salt in a bowl, then sprinkle evenly over the nuts. Roast for about 5 minutes, until warmed through but not coloured.

Whisk the egg whites until stiff in a separate bowl, then fold in the sugar to make a meringue. Pour over the hot nuts and mix well to combine. Return to the oven for another 8–10 minutes, until fragrant but not coloured. Stir the nuts occasionally while they are cooling to prevent them from sticking.

To serve, arrange in bowls and allow guests to help themselves.

Parmesan cheese straws

Make these up to 2 days in advance and store in an airtight container at room temperature. Alternatively, make and freeze up to 1 month in advance. Defrost and crisp in a preheated oven at 200°C/400°F/gas 6 for 3 minutes.

Serves 4–6

100 g (4 oz) plain flour, plus extra for dusting
75 g (3 oz) butter, diced and chilled
1 egg yolk
100 g (4 oz) Gruyère cheese, grated
pinch cayenne pepper
1 egg, beaten with 1 tablespoon water
2 tablespoons freshly grated Parmesan
salt and freshly ground black pepper
sour cream and chive dip or guacamole (page 116), to serve (optional)

Place the flour in a food processor with the butter, egg yolk and cheese. Season to taste and add the cayenne pepper. Pulse until the mixture forms a firm pastry. Turn out onto a lightly floured surface and knead lightly until smooth.

Roll out the pastry to a 5 mm (¼ inch) thickness. Cut into strips about 1 cm (½ inch) wide and 7 ½ cm (3 inches) long. This amount should make about 30 straws in total. Place 2 cm (¾ inch) apart on baking sheets that have been lined with non-stick parchment paper. Chill for at least 30 minutes to firm up or up to 24 hours is fine.

Preheat the oven to 180°C/350°F/gas 4. Brush the pastry straws with the beaten egg mixture and sprinkle with the Parmesan. Bake for 12–15 minutes, until crisp and golden brown. Transfer to a wire rack to cool.

To serve, arrange on plates with or without dips.

Dill splits with smoked salmon

For the best results, cover the cooked scones immediately with a clean tea towel as they cool on the wire rack. This helps them to stay moist and fluffy. Prepare the scones up to 1 day in advance and store in an airtight container at room temperature. They also freeze very well for up to 1 month.

Serves 4–6

175 g (6 oz) plain flour, plus extra for dusting
pinch salt
1 heaped teaspoon baking powder
40 g (1 ½ oz) unsalted butter
1 tablespoon chopped fresh dill, plus tiny sprigs to garnish
about 120 ml (4 fl oz) buttermilk
120 ml (4 fl oz) crème fraîche
1 tablespoon horseradish sauce
150 g (5 oz) organic smoked salmon slices (such as Simply Better Dunnes Stores)
salt and coarsely ground black pepper

Preheat the oven to 220°C/425°F/gas 7. Sift the flour, a good pinch of salt and baking powder into a bowl. Rub in the butter and stir in the dill, then make a well in the centre and add enough of the buttermilk to mix to a soft dough.

Knead the dough briefly on a lightly floured surface, then roll out to a 1 cm (½ inch) thickness and stamp out ten 5 cm (2 inch) rounds using a fluted cutter. This dough should make about 20 rounds in total. Arrange slightly apart on a non-stick baking sheet dusted with flour and bake for 8–10 minutes, until well risen and golden brown. Cover with a clean tea towel and leave to cool on a wire rack.

To serve, combine the crème fraîche with the horseradish sauce in a bowl, then cut the salmon into 2 ½ cm (1 inch) wide pieces. Split the scones in half and divide the crème fraîche mixture among them. Place a piece of salmon on each one and add a sprinkling of pepper.

Sticky honey and soy sesame cocktail sausages

I just never seem to be able to make enough of these. Fortunately, they take just minutes to make and seconds to demolish. You have been warned! Don't forget to hand around a separate dish for used cocktail sticks.

Serves 4–6

20 cocktail sausages, about 350 g (12 oz) in total
2 tablespoons hoisin sauce
2 teaspoons dark soy sauce
2 teaspoons runny honey
1 tablespoon sesame seeds

Preheat the oven to 200°C/400°F/gas 6. Place the sausages in a single layer in a non-stick roasting tin. Mix together the hoisin sauce, soy sauce and honey in a bowl and pour over the sausages, turning to coat.

Bake the sausages for 20 minutes, then drain off any excess fat and sprinkle over the sesame seeds. Cook for another 15 minutes or until golden and sticky.

To serve, arrange on a warmed plate skewered with cocktail sticks.

Chocolate fondue

Tradition states that if you drop your fruit into the fondue you must kiss the person opposite you. If you want to serve this individually, skewer a mixture of fruits for each person and serve with a small dish of the chocolate fondue on each plate.

Serves 4–6

300 ml (½ pint) cream
50 ml (2 fl oz) milk
1 vanilla pod
450 g (1 lb) plain chocolate, broken into squares (minimum 55% cocoa solids)
1 banana
3 apples
1 small pineapple
150 g (5 oz) strawberries
100 g (4 oz) marshmallows
50 g (2 oz) sponge fingers

Place the cream and milk in a small pan. Split the vanilla pod lengthways and scrape the seeds into the pan. Slowly heat until just at boiling point. Remove from the heat and stir in the chocolate. Keep the fondue warm by sitting the pan within a larger pan of hand-hot water.

Cut the fruit into large slices or chunks, depending on the type of fruit. Leave the strawberries whole.

To serve, remove the fondue to a heatproof bowl and place in the centre of the table with the fruit, marshmallows and sponge fingers arranged in small dishes around it, then allow each person to dip one piece of fruit, marshmallow or sponge finger at a time into the fondue.

Movie
night

Chilli popcorn

This recipe could also be made using a microwave. Simply place all the ingredients for the chilli butter in a heatproof bowl and cook on full power for 30–40 seconds, until melted and just bubbling. Set aside. Cook a bag of microwavable popcorn according to packet instructions, then immediately pour over the chilli butter, shaking the bag to ensure an even coating. Tip into a bowl to serve.

Serves 4–6

50 g (2 oz) butter
1 garlic clove, crushed
½ teaspoon dried chilli flakes
2 teaspoons hot curry paste or powder
2 tablespoons sunflower oil
75 g (3 oz) popcorn kernels
salt and freshly ground black pepper

Melt the butter in a small pan and add the garlic, chilli and curry paste or powder, stirring to combine. Season with ½ teaspoon each of salt and pepper and keep warm over a low heat.

Heat the oil in a large pan until very hot, almost smoking. Add the popcorn kernels, and as it starts to pop, cover with a lid. Cook for 2–3 minutes, shaking the pan occasionally until the corn stops popping. Quickly pour over the chilli butter, shaking the pan to ensure it gets evenly distributed.

To serve, tip into bowls and hand around to guests.

Cheesy nachos with avocado and sweetcorn salsa

This is wicked comfort food at its best, perfect for a night in with a good movie. Make sure you follow with one of my ice cream suggestions on page 192. Jalapeño chillies are the green sliced ones that come in jars. They pack quite a punch, so leave them out if you don't like your food too hot.

Serves 4–6

100 g (4 oz) canned or frozen sweetcorn kernels
1 ripe tomato, seeded and diced
1 small ripe avocado, peeled, stoned and diced
4 spring onions, thinly sliced
25 g (1 oz) sliced jalapeño chillies, drained and chopped (from a jar) (optional)
175 g (6 oz) packet tortilla chips
3–4 tablespoons sour cream
25 g (1 oz) Cheddar, grated
salt and freshly ground black pepper

Preheat the oven to 200°C/400°F/gas 6. If using frozen sweetcorn, place in a pan of boiling salted water and cook for a few minutes until just tender, then drain and refresh under cold running water. Place the sweetcorn in a large bowl with the tomato, avocado, spring onions and jalapeño chillies, if using. Stir to combine and season to taste.

Tip the tortilla chips into an ovenproof dish and scatter the avocado and sweetcorn salsa on top. Spoon over the sour cream and finish with the Cheddar. Bake for about 10 minutes, until the Cheddar has melted and is bubbling.

To serve, bring the dish of cheesy nachos straight to the table and allow guests to help themselves.

Mini hot dogs with caramelised onions

This is a real kids' favourite but always goes down well with adults too. Of course, you could use frankfurters and simply drizzle over the barbecue sauce, but I prefer good-quality sausages from a craft butcher or speciality range from the supermarket.

Serves 4–6

6 tablespoons tomato ketchup
1 tablespoon dark soy sauce
1 tablespoon sweet chilli sauce (optional)
1 teaspoon Dijon mustard
1 teaspoon clear honey
12 good-quality pork sausages
1 large onion, halved and cut into thick slices
2 tablespoons sunflower oil
12 mini hot dog buns or sub rolls

Preheat the grill. Mix together the tomato ketchup and soy sauce with the sweet chilli sauce, if using, and the mustard and honey in a small bowl. Place the sausages in a non-metallic dish. Pour over half the barbecue sauce and spread it on the sausages. Grill the sausages for 8–10 minutes, until golden brown and cooked through, turning and basting occasionally.

Meanwhile, separate the onion into pieces. Heat the oil in a frying pan and sauté the onion for 8–10 minutes or until softened and lightly golden. Drain on kitchen paper.

To serve, lay the sausages in the bottom halves of the hot dog buns or sub rolls and scatter over the caramelised onion, then drizzle over the rest of the barbecue sauce and place on warmed plates.

Lemonade float

When I was a child, there was no better treat than a bowl of ice cream, so next time you feel like indulging yourself, don't fight the desire – whip up one of these floats that can literally be made in minutes.

Serves 4–6

300–450 ml (½–¾ pint) exotic fruit juice
4–6 scoops vanilla ice cream
200–300 ml (7 fl oz–½ pint) sparkling traditional lemonade
lightly crushed Smarties, to decorate

Half-fill tall glasses with the exotic fruit juice. Add a scoop of vanilla ice cream and fill up with sparkling traditional lemonade.

To serve, decorate each glass with lightly crushed Smarties.

Vanilla ice cream with espresso and biscotti

The seductively rich flavour and smooth, velvety texture of this dessert will test even the strongest of wills. We always keep a tub of vanilla ice cream in the freezer for times when there's no avoiding that craving for something sweet.

Serves 4–6

500 ml (18 fl oz) tub vanilla ice cream (good-quality)
4–6 shots hot freshly brewed espresso coffee
100 g (4 oz) biscotti, roughly smashed

Scoop half the vanilla ice cream into glass coffee cups and pour a shot of espresso over each one. Scoop the remaining ice cream on top.

To serve, sprinkle each glass with roughly smashed biscotti.

192

LIMERICK
COUNTY LIBRARY

Index

Notes

Notes

Notes

Notes

Notes